Everyman, I will go with thee,
and be thy guide

Josephus

THE LIFE OF HEROD
from the *Jewish Antiquities* of Josephus

Translated from the Greek by
JOHN GREGORY

EVERYMAN
J. M. DENT · LONDON
CHARLES E. TUTTLE
VERMONT

Translation from the Greek © John Gregory 1998
Introduction and other critical material © J. M. Dent 1998

This edition first published in Everyman Paperbacks in 1998

J. M. Dent
Orion Publishing Group
Orion House, 5 Upper St Martin's Lane,
London WC2H 9EA
and
Charles E. Tuttle Co., Inc.
28 South Main Street,
Rutland, Vermont 05701, USA

Printed in Great Britain by The Guernsey Press, Channel Islands

British Library Cataloguing-in-Publication Data
is available on request.

ISBN 0 460 87646 5

CONTENTS

CHRONOLOGY OF HEROD'S LIFE

Year	History of the Jews	Events in Roman World
72 BC	Birth of Herod	
48	Hyrcanus and Antipater (Herod's father) assist Caesar against Ptolemy XIII	Battle of Pharsalus (9 August); Caesar defeats Pompey and pursues him to Egypt
47	Caesar confirms Hyrcanus as high priest and ethnarch and appoints Antipater procurator of Judaea; Herod made governor of Galilee; his summons before the Sanhedrin	Sextus Caesar made governor of Syria
46		Murder of Sextus Caesar; Bassus controls Syria
45	Herod and Phasael reinforce the Caesarcans at Apamea	
44	Herod collects tribute for Cassius	Murder of Julius Caesar (15 March); Cassius takes control of Syria
43	Herod made governor of Coele-Syria by Cassius; Antipater murdered by Malichus; Herod avenges his father's death	
42	Herod expels Antigonus from Judaea	The Battle of Philippi (October); deaths of Cassius and Brutus
41	Herod defends himself before Antony in Bithynia; Antony restores Jewish captives and property for Hyrcanus; Antony appoints Herod and Phasael tetrarchs, massacres Jewish deputies	

Year	History of the Jews	Events in Roman World
40 BC	Parthians install Antigonus as king; captivity of Hyrcanus and death of Phasael; Herod escapes from Judaea and appeals to Antony in Rome; Herod in Rome proclaimed king of the Jews	The Parthians invade Syria
39	Herod and Silo besiege Antigonus in Jerusalem	
38	Herod captures the bandits of Arbela, and reconquers Galilee; rescues Antony's allies from the Parthians, and is welcomed by Antony at Samosata; avenges Joseph's death at Jericho	
37	Herod and Sosius besiege Jerusalem (spring); Herod marries Mariamme I; capture of Jerusalem, execution of Antigonus and other opponents	
36	Hyrcanus returns from Parthia	
35	Appointment of Aristobulus III as high priest, and his murder	
34	Antony in Laodicea is reconciled with Herod; execution of Joseph, Salome's husband; Cleopatra given part of Herod's territory, and visits Judaea	
32/1	Herod's war with the Nabataean Arabs	
31	Herod sides with Octavian	Battle of Actium, defeat of Antony and Cleopatra by Octavian (2 September); Octavian (Caesar Octavian) sole ruler of the Roman world
30	Execution of Hyrcanus; Octavian receives Herod in Rhodes and Egypt and extends his dominions	

Year	History of the Jews	Events in Roman World
29 BC	Execution of Mariamme	
28?	Execution of Alexandra	
27?	Rebuilding of Samaria (Sebaste) begun	Octavian given name Augustus
25?	Execution of Costobarus and the sons of Baba; quadrennial athletic games founded in Jerusalem	
25/4?	Famine and plague in Judaea; Herod builds his royal palace, marries Mariamme II	
23/2	Alexander and Aristobulus sent to Rome for their education; Augustus gives Herod Trachonitis, Batanaea and Auranitis; the building of Caesarea begun	
20	Augustus gives Herod the territory of Zenodorus; Pheroras made tetrarch of Peraea	
20/19	Herod remits one-third of the taxes, demands an oath of loyalty; the rebuilding of the Temple begun	
18/17	Herod brings home Mariamme's sons from Rome	
15	Agrippa visits Herod in Jerusalem	
14	Herod with Agrippa in Asia, defends Jewish rights; remits a quarter of the taxes; Antipater arrives at court	
13	Antipater sent to Rome	
12	Herod in Rome accuses Alexander and Aristobulus before Augustus	
10?	Caesarea dedicated; Alexander imprisoned; Archelaus of Cappadocia reconciles Herod with his sons	

Year	History of the Jews	Events in Roman World
9? BC	Herod's campaign against the Nabataeans	
8/7	Alexander and Aristobulus accused of high treason, condemned and executed; execution of suspected Pharisees	
6?	Antipater goes to Rome; Herod's first will	
5	Death of Pheroras; Antipater returns to Judaea, is tried and imprisoned; Herod's second will	
4	Herod punishes Judas and Matthias and their disciples; execution of Antipater; Herod's final will; death of Herod	

CHRONOLOGY OF JOSEPHUS'S LIFE

Year	Life and Times
AD 37/8	Joseph ben Matthias born in Jerusalem.
53/4	Aged 16, studies the observances of the Pharisees, Sadducees and Essenes; begins three years of discipleship in the desert with the ascetic Bannus
54	Accession of the emperor Nero
56/7	Aged 19, Josephus returns to Jerusalem and participates in public life; attaches himself to the Pharisees in his public life
63/4	Travels to Rome to secure the release of imprisoned Jewish priests; secures help of Poppaea Sabina, Nero's wife; returns to Judaea
66	The start of the Jewish War; Jewish forces rout the army of Cestius Gallus, governor of Syria; Josephus sent to command Galilee
67	Vespasian besieges and captures Jotapata; Josephus escapes and surrenders to the Romans
67–9	Josephus held in custody
68	The death of Nero
68–9	The year of the Four Emperors; Vespasian proclaimed emperor (summer 69), the first of the Flavian dynasty
70	Titus besieges and demolishes Jerusalem; Josephus, in the Roman camp, acts as mediator
71	Josephus (now Flavius) resides in Rome, under imperial patronage and protection
c.73	Publishes Aramaic edition of the *Jewish War*
75–9	Publishes Greek edition of the *Jewish War*
79–81	Titus emperor
81–96	Domitian emperor
93/4	Josephus completes the *Jewish Antiquities* and his *Life* (autobiography)
post 93/4	Publishes *Against Apion* (a defence of Judaism)

INTRODUCTION

Josephus was an upper-class priest from Jerusalem who under-
went great changes in the course of his life and ended as a
literary figure in the imperial court in Rome. The chief impact
on his tumultuous career was his participation in the revolt of
the Jews against Rome in AD 66–70, a revolt which ended in
the destruction of the great Temple in Jerusalem, up to that time
the main spiritual focus of Judaism. During the war Josephus
was briefly a general on the side of the Jewish rebels but, after a
dream which he interpreted as a divine message, he surrendered
in AD 67 to the Romans. Treated at first as a prisoner of war,
in AD 69 he was freed by the new Roman emperor Vespasian in
recognition of his prophetic abilities which (it was alleged) had
led him in AD 67 to foretell Vespasian's rise to supreme power
at a time when the latter, at that time simply general in
command of the Roman army in Judaea, could hardly have
even thought of the possibility. After AD 70 Josephus went with
Vespasian to Rome and took up residence in the house originally occupied by Vespasian's own family. Josephus received
an income from lands in Judaea granted to him by the emperor,
but so far as is known he remained in Rome for the rest of his
life.

As a man of leisure Josephus took to writing history. His
account of the *Jewish War* in seven books, completed by the
late 70s, depicted the rebellion in which he had participated as
a conflict on a grand scale; as the title of the work suggests, the
perspective of the historian came essentially from the Roman
side. The twenty books of the *Jewish Antiquities*, from which
the *Life of Herod* included in this volume has been excerpted,
was composed between AD 79 and 93. They give the whole
story of the Jews from the beginning to AD 66. In around AD
93 Josephus also published his *Life*, an autobiographical defence
of his own behaviour during the revolt in defiance of his critics,
and at some time in the years following he wrote a response to

pagan attacks on Jews and Judaism in a work in two books now entitled *Against Apion*. This voluminous output is extant because Josephus's writings were preserved by early Christians, who found in them invaluable evidence about the background to the life and career of Jesus. The extant Jewish tradition from the centuries following Josephus's death is silent about him and his writings, in part probably simply because the rabbis who preserved this tradition used Hebrew and Aramaic and were apparently unaware of most Judaeo-Greek literature. Josephus refers in passing to further literary projects, but whether he in fact composed any works apart from those that survive is unknown.

It has been traditional to berate Josephus for his change of sides during the war, but it may be more appropriate when considering his qualities as a writer to draw attention to his extraordinary bravery in writing in praise of Jews and Judaism in the atmosphere of the court in Rome, where the main plank of imperial propaganda after AD 70 was the victory over the Jews. His triumphant capture of Jerusalem was used by Vespasian as justification for his seizure of power in Rome in a bloody civil war: the honour accorded to successful generals for expanding the empire was a traditional means to political eminence in Roman society. In any case Josephus's conscious decision to write within the Graeco-Roman genre of historiography invited readers to judge his work by the accuracy of his narration about the past. It is clear that some of his readers took up the invitation, since the complaints of critics countered in his *Life* revolve around the alleged falsehoods in his earlier account of his career in the *Jewish War*.

The *Life of Herod* included in this volume has been excerpted from Books XIV to XVII of the *Jewish Antiquities*. Josephus seems to have modelled his great work on the *Roman Antiquities* of Dionysius of Halicarnassus written some hundred years earlier. Dionysius was, like Josephus, an eastern provincial writing in Rome in the Greek language, and Josephus may have hoped to show by the comparison that the Jews were a people as important and ancient as the Romans. The desire to fill twenty books provided Josephus with some difficulties: the Bible provided plentiful material for the first ten books but post-biblical Jewish history was scantily recorded, and Josephus was sometimes reduced to filling his pages with material only marginally relevant to the history of the Jewish people, such as the complexities of court life in imperial Rome, which takes up a good proportion of Book XIX. Hence the eagerness with which Josephus exploited the detailed narrative available to him about Herod the Great.

Josephus's main source for this narrative was the court historian of Herod, a certain Nicolas of Damascus. Nicolas was one of a number of non-Jewish intellectuals who were attracted by the wealth, power and glamour of Herod to join his circle, perhaps by 20 BC and certainly by 14 BC, since after that date he was entrusted by Herod with a number of delicate diplomatic duties which are duly recorded by Josephus in the *Antiquities*. His intellectual interests were apparently quite broad, and his output prodigious: his compositions included philosophical works, a study of paradoxical customs, and possibly tragedies and comedies, in addition to the great historical work in 144 books from which, it may reasonably be surmised, Josephus took his information about Herod. Nicolas's voluminous *History* traced the story of the world from ancient times, with vastly increased detail as he approached the events of his own lifetime. Little survives from this massive output, but some impression of those parts of the *History* which dealt with contemporary matters can be deduced from the fragments preserved from Nicolas's *Autobiography*.

Nicolas seems never to have fully understood Judaism or Jewish society, for his personal loyalty to Herod did not lead to a commitment to his adopted community. Before his career in Herod's court he may have been tutor to the children of Antony and Cleopatra in Egypt, and on Herod's death in 4 BC he took the opportunity of a public appearance in Rome as advocate of one of Herod's sons in the dispute over the succession to commend himself to Augustus, so that his final years were spent in or near the imperial court in the capital city. Nicolas belongs to a type, quite common in the early Roman empire, of the wandering Greek intellectual, prepared to offer his services whenever opportunity offered itself. He was by no means unique among such intellectuals in his origins from Syria.

Josephus's other sources must have included an oral tradition about Herod, who had after all died only forty years or so before Josephus's birth: at *Ant.*15.425 there is an explicit reference to a story 'which our fathers have handed down to us'. At

*Ant.*15.174 Josephus refers to the *Memoirs* written by Herod himself, but not in a way to encourage the view that he had seen and used them. Elsewhere (*Ant.*15.9–10) Josephus mentions in passing the views of Strabo, a Greek historian and geographer who lived and wrote in Herod's time, but it is unlikely that he provided a major source. It is probable that, if Josephus had another written account at his disposal in addition to the writings of Nicolas, it was hostile to Herod: this would help to explain the contradictory assessments of Herod's character and motives scattered throughout the narrative.

Herod the Great, ruler of Judaea from 37 BC to his death in 4 BC, is best known today for his brief appearance in the Christian traditions about the birth of Jesus and as the originator of the monumental rebuilding of the Temple in Jerusalem, but Josephus's account of his tumultuous career preserves more details about his grandiose achievements and complex personality than for almost any other politician of his time apart from the Roman emperor.

Herod was one of the most colourful and influential figures of the political world of the early Roman empire. His success was only to a limited extent a product of his origins. He was the son of Antipater, an Idumaean adviser to the Jewish king Hyrcanus, whose own Hasmonaean dynasty had controlled Judaea since the mid-second century BC. Antipater's influence over Hyrcanus was at least in part encouraged by the fact he was not a Judaean Jew: the Idumaeans had been converted *en masse* to Judaism in the 120s BC and their status within Judaism was still treated as insecure by some Judaeans even two and a half centuries later. Hyrcanus might therefore trust his Idumaean minister to be loyal to him, for Antipater lacked the social prestige which could have brought him power in Judaea in his own right. The same social disqualifications applied equally to Herod, as he grew up on the fringes of the Hasmonaean court. He was indeed even further disadvantaged, for his mother was a Nabataean Arab – it is not even recorded whether she ever converted to Judaism – and the bloody ruthlessness he displayed in his early political career did not endear him to the inhabitants of Judaea.

Herod's appointment as king of Judaea in 40 BC, albeit for the first three years without any power in his own kingdom, was thus against all expectations, including his own

(*Ant.*14.386). The cause of his elevation lay not in the politics of Judaea or the aspirations of the Jews but in the machinations of Roman aristocrats. On the Ides of March 44 BC Julius Caesar was murdered in Rome by disaffected senators. For the next thirteen years the Mediterranean world became the arena for wars on a massive scale in which these and other aristocrats battled, until Caesar's adopted son Octavian defeated Mark Antony at the Battle of Actium (31 BC) and emerged supreme, receiving in 27 BC the name 'Augustus' in recognition of his role in achieving the peace which had by then finally come to the Roman world. Within this wider power game Herod was only a pawn. Throughout his life ultimate control always rested in Rome, a fact amply reflected in Josephus's account.

After Caesar's murder Judaea fell at first into the hands of his assassins, Brutus and Cassius (43 BC). Cassius was desperate for money for the war against Mark Antony and Herod's success in raising funds for him was noted, so that after the defeat of the liberators by Mark Antony at the Battle of Philippi in 42 BC it was natural for the victor to seek help from the energetic young supporter of his erstwhile opponent. Antony's patronage of Herod was to last to the end of the former's life, but in 40 BC Judaea was invaded along with other parts of the Levant by the Parthians, a state based in Mesopotamia and Iran whose leaders took advantage of Roman disarray to avenge earlier Roman incursions into their territory. The Parthians deposed the Hasmonaean Hyrcanus, the long-time patron of Antipater and more recently also of Herod, and Herod fled to Rome to seek help. In Rome Antony persuaded the Senate to proclaim Herod king of Judaea, in the hope that a young man of such energy and ambition might take steps for such a reward to recover the territory from the Parthians. Following the proclamation Herod joined the consuls and other magistrates of Rome in a sacrifice to Jupiter on the Capitol (*Ant.*14.388–9) a symbolic reflection of his ambiguous Judaism which helped to reinforce his uneasy relationship with his Jewish subjects in later years.

Herod did not himself possess any military force with which to win his kingdom, and there followed three years in which he endeavoured with little success to persuade Roman generals to attack Judaea on his behalf. When Sosius finally took Jerusalem in the summer of 37 BC Herod was hard put to restrain him and his soldiers from sacking his new capital. Heavy bribery induced Sosius to withdraw, but Herod was not to enjoy his kingdom in tranquillity for many years. Apart from opposition by his Jewish subjects, his main concern was the ambition of Cleopatra, queen of Egypt and mistress of Mark Antony. Her hostility was warded off by exceptional diplomatic skills, which were again taxed to the utmost when Antony and Cleopatra were defeated by Octavian in 31 BC. Herod did not deny to Octavian his previous loyalty to Mark Antony, but he declared that he would prove as loyal to the victor as he had been to his enemy (*Ant.*15.189–95). The tactic seems to have been successful.

For the rest of his life and career, Herod kept steadfastly to his loyalty to Octavian (known from 27 BC as 'Augustus' but generally designated by Josephus as 'Caesar', the family name he had inherited from Julius Caesar). Apart from one misunderstanding (see below), Herod seems to have retained the confidence of the autocrat. From the point of view of Augustus, Herod's reliance on his goodwill provided insurance against disobedience. Such use of client rulers – 'friendly kings' – was a common characteristic of Roman imperial administration in this period: references to client kings in other regions, and the delicate relationships between them and Herod and his family, crop up frequently in Josephus's history.

Herod ruled Judaea with an iron grip, symbolised by the erection of numerous fortresses within his kingdom for domination of his dominion. Despite occasional attempts to curry favour from his Jewish subjects, he seems to have been reconciled to constant hostility, occasionally suppressed with bloody ferocity. He had greater success in winning admiration and support on the wider international scene, where his generous munificence was widely appreciated. In relations with other states his only serious difficulties after 31 BC lay in his often complex symbiosis with the neighbouring Nabataean Arabs, who inhabited southern Transjordan, and his brief invasion of Nabataean territory in *c.*9 BC was the cause of the one breach in his friendship with Augustus.

But the main focus of his reign, and the main source of his troubles, lay in his own court, and especially within his own extensive family. The problems began from the start of his reign, but they became acute from 29 BC when he executed on suspicion of treason his Hasmonaean wife Mariamme. From about 15 BC, as he neared the end of his life and speculation about the succession was rampant, the court became almost wholly given over to intrigue, plot and rumour. The last decade of his rule witnessed a bloodbath among his sons which became proverbial even in distant Rome, hence the tag that 'it is better to be Herod's pig than Herod's son'. (The joke is preserved in Latin but must originally have been in Greek: the Greek word for pig is *hus*, the word for son is *huios*.)

The *Life of Herod* by Josephus presented in this volume never existed in antiquity as a separate work, and the unity of the material here excerpted derives mainly from the subject matter. The process of extracting the *Life of Herod* from the *Antiquities* has necessarily produced some infelicities for the new reader in the opening pages. Herod was introduced by Josephus on to the stage of wider Jewish history only gradually, since his role during the 40s BC was only minor, and for the narrative up to 37 BC (the end of Book XIV) Herod shares the limelight with Antigonus, the last ruler of the ancient Hasmonaean line, whose demise is lamented by Josephus with much energy. (Josephus himself was descended through one branch of his family from a Hasmonaean princess, a matter of great pride, as emerges from his own *Life*.)

As the narrative progresses after Herod's accession to power, it focuses more and more on Herod's friends, on his close family, and on the increasingly lonely king himself. This focus is a product both of Josephus's source of evidence – primarily Nicolas – and his use of techniques characteristic of Graeco-Roman historiography. Thus he seeks to produce an emotional response in his readers by describing with empathy the feelings of his characters, and he gives vent to fine displays of rhetoric in his report of the speeches made about his family's failings by or on behalf of Herod in the cases heard before Augustus in Rome: like all such speeches in ancient historical works, they will have been written up by the historian to describe what was appropriate rather than what was actually said, although Josephus may well have borrowed some of the rhetoric found in the orations of Nicolas from Nicolas's own account of his achievements.

It was also characteristic of the genre for the historian to provide a moral commentary on the characters in his history, and this Josephus does quite liberally, sometimes with pious asides about the role of the divine in punishing wickedness. The incentive for such comments seems to arise on occasion from the discrepancies between the favourable picture of Herod's behaviour inherited from Nicolas and Josephus's own less charitable view. Some other features of Josephus's historiographical technique may not emerge entirely from the translation. One of the prime tasks of the Greek historian was the recording of his material in an appropriate literary style. Josephus was painfully aware of his inadequacy in the use of Greek, attempting to excuse himself by the fact that he was not a native speaker of the language, but he tried to compensate by imitating the Attic style, the language of classical Athens, with sometimes convoluted, pretentious and inelegant results.

The historical accuracy of the *Life* is probably quite high, in so far as Josephus's sources enabled him to present the truth: Nicolas undoubtedly put a favourable gloss on his description of the less savoury episodes in his patron's career, as Josephus states explicitly (*Ant.*16.184–6), but he also provided the information with which Josephus could give a counter-judgement, since he had an insider's knowledge of rumour and gossip within the royal court. Comparison between Josephus's account in the *Antiquities* and his much shorter narration of the same events in his earlier history of the *Jewish War*, where he lacked space to comment on the significance of the story he told, reveals numerous minor variations, particularly in chronology, but no major discrepancies: most differences are best explained as the result of over-compression and haste in the *Jewish War*, since in that account the career of Herod featured only as a minor element of the causes of the war of AD 66–70.

The *Antiquities* were composed for a non-Jewish readership in order to emphasise the significance of Jewish history from ancient times. Such a motive may have encouraged Josephus to make undue claims of the importance of Herod on the world stage, although Josephus's judgement is in general supported by non-Jewish writers of the time and ensuing generations. Josephus himself refers to the possibility of political pressures on him from surviving descendants of Herod, but his claim to have put truth above their favour (*Ant.*16.187) seems justified, since some of his comments on the character of his subject are fairly damning. If he is to be faulted as a historian it may be more just to point to a certain carelessness; it has been suggested that he was growing tired as he neared the completion of his great work. Thus material is sometimes thrown together in a rather arbitrary and confused fashion. In the *Life of Herod* this tendency is most noticeable in the earlier parts of the story, when Josephus could not follow the narrative structure of Nicolas; the beginning of the *Life of Herod* is too compressed for easy comprehension.

For the Greek text translated here Benedictus Niese's edition of Josephus's works, published in Berlin between 1885 and 1895, has been used, supplemented by reference to more recent textual criticism. In those places where Josephus inserted into his history material quite unconnected to Herod, the text has been omitted; such omissions are clearly marked in the translation. The Greek manuscripts of Josephus's works were frequently copied in the Middle Ages and the oldest extant manuscripts come from the ninth–eleventh centuries. These manuscripts can occasionally be corrected from the testimony of earlier quotations of Josephus in the writings of the Church Fathers. The translation of Josephus's works was already begun by Christians in antiquity. By far the most popular and widespread English version is included in *The Genuine Works of Flavius Josephus* by William Whiston, published in 1737. Otherwise these books of the *Jewish Antiquities* are available in English by Ralph Marcus in volumes 7 and 8 of the parallel text edition published by the Loeb Classical Library in 1943 and 1963.

The *Life of Herod* is not great literature, but it is a gripping historical account composed with passionate involvement and derived from the evidence of eye-witnesses. The *Life* provides an extraordinary insight into the political machinations and emotional turmoil of a despot whose grandiose aims were achieved at the expense of personal happiness.

MARTIN GOODMAN

THE LIFE OF HEROD

BOOK XIV

In the spring of 47 BC Julius Caesar sailed from Egypt to Syria, where he confirmed the position of Hyrcanus II as high priest and ethnarch of the Jews and appointed Antipater, Herod's father, as his procurator.

Governor of Galilee

156 After settling the affairs of Syria, Caesar sailed away. Antipater, who had escorted Caesar out of Syria, returned to Judaea and at once rebuilt the wall demolished by Pompey;* and he travelled the country putting down disturbances by a combination of threats and persuasion.

157 He promised that those who were loyal to Hyrcanus would live in peace, secure in the enjoyment of their own possessions, but warned that if they pinned their hopes on revolution and were counting on the gains it might bring them, then they would find him their master instead of their protector, and Hyrcanus a tyrant instead of a king. They would also make bitter enemies of their rulers, the Romans and Caesar, who would not tolerate the overthrow of the man they had placed in power. While saying this Antipater began to organise the country on his own initiative.

158 Realising that Hyrcanus was dull-witted and indolent, he appointed his eldest son Phasael* to be governor of Jerusalem and its environs, and entrusted Galilee to his second son Herod, who was then only fifteen* and still

159 extremely young. But his youth proved no handicap, for Herod was a young man of brave spirit and at once found an opportunity to show his mettle. Learning that the bandit chief Ezekias was overrunning the borders of Syria with a large horde, he caught him and put him to death

160 together with many of his men. It was an exploit that won

him the admiration of the Syrians for clearing their land of the banditry from which they had longed to be delivered; and he was celebrated in their towns and villages as the man who had brought them peace and the secure enjoyment of their possessions. As a further consequence he came to the notice of Sextus Caesar, a relative of the great Caesar and governor of Syria.*

161   His brother Phasael, meanwhile, inspired by Herod's achievements with the spirit of emulation, and keenly conscious of his fame, was ambitious to match him in public esteem, and enhanced his popularity with the people of Jerusalem, while keeping the city under his personal control, by managing its affairs with discretion and avoid-
162   ing any abuse of his authority. Antipater, as a result, was revered by the nation as if he were king, and received honours befitting a head of state; yet the glory that reflected on him in no way diminished his friendship and loyalty towards Hyrcanus, as so often happens.

163   But when the leading Jews saw how Antipater and his sons were growing in power, with the support of the nation and the revenues they received from Judaea and the personal wealth of Hyrcanus, they became resentful of
164   him. Antipater, indeed, had also formed a friendship with the Roman generals, by persuading Hyrcanus to send them money but then appropriating the gift and sending it
165   instead as his own. When Hyrcanus heard about it he was very pleased, and not in the least concerned. The Jewish leaders, however, were frightened by what they saw of Herod's aggressive and reckless character, and his lust for autocratic power, and they now came to Hyrcanus and accused Antipater publicly. 'How much longer,' they said, 'are you going to remain indifferent to what is happening? Can you not see that Antipater and his sons have assumed the royal power, while you are king in name alone? Do
166   not ignore this threat, nor imagine that your careless disregard for yourself and your kingdom protects you from danger. Antipater and his sons are no longer your viceroys in the government, and you should not deceive yourself by supposing it: it is openly acknowledged that
167   they have absolute power. Look at his son Herod, for example. He killed Ezekias and many of his men in

contravention of our Law, which forbids the taking of a man's life, however wicked, unless he has first been sentenced to death by the Sanhedrin* – and he dared to do this without authority from you.'

168 Hyrcanus was swayed by what he heard, and the flames of his anger were fanned by the mothers of Herod's murdered victims, who gathered every day in the Temple and kept appealing to the king and the people to bring Herod to account for his actions before the Sanhedrin.

169 Moved by their pleas, Hyrcanus summoned Herod to stand trial for the crimes of which he was accused; and Herod came. He was advised by his father not to enter the city as a private individual but with the security of a bodyguard, and after making arrangements in Galilee to protect his interests he brought with him a military escort just adequate for his journey. With a larger body of men he might have appeared to pose a threat to Hyrcanus, but he was unwilling to go entirely unarmed and unprotected.

170 So Herod came to stand trial. Sextus, however, the governor of Syria, wrote to Hyrcanus requesting his acquittal, and backed up his request with threats in case he should refuse; and the letter gave Hyrcanus, who loved Herod like a son, a pretext for releasing him unharmed from the Sanhedrin.

171 When Herod took his stand in the Sanhedrin with his bodyguard, he disconcerted the whole assembly, and none of those who had denounced him before his arrival now

172 dared to accuse him. Instead, there was silence and they were uncertain how to proceed. While they hesitated, a man named Samaias, who had too much integrity to give way to fear, stood up and spoke. 'Fellow councillors and King,' he said, 'I can recall no previous occasion when a defendant summoned to stand trial before you has presented such an appearance as this, and I doubt if you can name a precedent. Anyone – whoever he may be – who comes to be judged before this Sanhedrin, presents an abject appearance, bearing himself like a frightened man dependent on your mercy, with dishevelled hair and black

173 attire. But Herod – fine man that he is! – though accused of murder and summoned on no less a charge, stands clothed in purple, his hair neatly set, and surrounded by

soldiers. If we condemn him as the law prescribes, he intends to kill us, and to save himself by outraging justice.

174 Yet it is not Herod whom I would blame on this account, for putting his own interest above the law, but you and the king for having given him such licence. Be assured, however, that God is great, and that this man, whom you are now willing to release to oblige Hyrcanus, will one day punish you, together with the king.'

175 He was not mistaken in his prophecy, for when Herod became king he put to death all the members of the Sanhedrin, including Hyrcanus himself, with the sole

176 exception of Samaias. Herod held him in high regard on account of his integrity, and because when he and Sosius later besieged the city Samaias advised the people to admit Herod, telling them that for their sins they had no power to escape him. Of these events we shall speak in their proper place.

177 When Hyrcanus saw that the Sanhedrin were resolved on Herod's destruction, he postponed the trial to another day* and sent secretly to Herod advising him to flee the

178 city, and so escape the danger he was in. Herod accordingly withdrew to Damascus, as if in flight from the king, and joined Sextus Caesar; and after securing his position he was determined that, if summoned again to stand trial before the Sanhedrin, he would refuse to comply. The

179 Sanhedrin reacted angrily and tried to convince Hyrcanus that it was against him that all Herod's movements were directed; but although he saw the threat, he was too

180 spineless and incompetent to take action. Herod, in return for a gift of money, was made governor of Coele-Syria* by Sextus, and Hyrcanus now began to fear that he would march against him – a fear that was soon realised when Herod advanced on him with his army, still furious with him because of the trial and his summons to give account of himself to the Sanhedrin.

181 However, he was dissuaded from attacking Jerusalem by his father Antipater and his brother, who went to meet him and checked his aggressive impulse, urging him to avoid a military engagement. The threat by itself, they said, was sufficient to intimidate Hyrcanus, and he ought not to proceed further against the man who had enabled

182 him to rise to his present position. While he might feel resentful at being summoned to stand trial, they begged him to remember his acquittal also and to be thankful for it: after facing the ugly alternative of condemnation he

183 would be wrong to begrudge his deliverance. He should reflect that, if it is God who turns the scales of war, then injustice weighs more heavily than an army, and in proposing to attack his king and companion, a generous benefactor who had done him no unkindness, he could have no assurance of victory. And as for his complaints, they said, Hyrcanus had dealt him only the barest hint of ill-treatment, and not of his own accord but through the influence of evil counsellors.

184 Herod yielded to these arguments, believing that he had satisfied his ambitions for the future by simply demonstrating his strength to the nation. Such was the state of affairs in Judaea.

Here Josephus interrupts his narrative to quote the texts of Roman decrees confirming the position of Hyrcanus, and his sons after him, as ethnarch and high priest, and granting privileges to the Jews of Palestine and Asia, including the right to observe the Sabbath and other religious customs, exemption from military service and freedom from taxation in a sabbatical year.

Herod Avenges his Father's Murder

268 It was about the same time that there was trouble in Syria, for the following reason. Caecilius Bassus, one of Pompey's supporters, formed a plot against Sextus Caesar, and after killing him and taking over his army made himself master of the country; and a major war broke out near Apamea when Caesar's generals led a force of cavalry and

269 infantry against him.* Antipater also sent them reinforcements with his sons, in recognition of the benefits they had received from Caesar, which he thought it his duty to

270 repay by avenging Sextus and exacting satisfaction from his murderer. As the war dragged on Murcus came from

Rome to succeed Sextus as governor, and Caesar was killed in the senate-house by Cassius, Brutus and the other conspirators, after holding power for three years and six months.* But this is related by other historians.

271   On the outbreak of the war that followed Caesar's death, the protagonists all dispersed to raise an army, and Cassius arrived in Syria to take command of the armies

272   around Apamea. After raising the siege, he effected a reconciliation between Bassus and Murcus, and then marched upon the cities, collecting arms and soldiers and imposing heavy tribute on them; and he was particularly severe on Judaea, from which he exacted seven hundred

273   talents of silver. In view of the fear and confusion that prevailed, Antipater divided the responsibility for collecting the tribute, giving each of his sons a portion to collect

274   and ordering others, including his enemy Malichus, to raise the rest of the money. Herod earned the special friendship of Cassius by being the first to raise the sum required of him, from the land of Galilee, believing it to be sound policy for him to begin to cultivate the friendship

275   of the Romans and secure their goodwill at the expense of others. The officials in the other cities, without exception, were sold as slaves, and Cassius reduced four cities to servitude on that occasion – Gophna and Emmaus, the most important, together with Lydda and Thamna. As for

276   Malichus, Cassius was so furious with him that he had resolved to take his life, and was only prevented from doing so when Hyrcanus sent him, through Antipater, a personal gift of a hundred talents.

277   But when Cassius left Judaea, Malichus plotted against Antipater, whose death he believed would help to secure Hyrcanus's power. Antipater, however, became aware of his intentions, and crossed the Jordan and recruited an army of both Arabs and native people. At this the

278   resourceful Malichus denied the plot and defended himself under oath to Antipater and his sons, by claiming that he would never have entertained such a notion with Phasael guarding Jerusalem and Herod in charge of the armoury, but would have seen it to be impracticable. So he became

279   reconciled with Antipater, and they settled their difference. The governor of Syria at this time was Murcus, who had

learned that Malichus was stirring up trouble in Judaea
and was on the point of putting him to death; but on the
plea of Antipater he spared him.

280   In saving Malichus, however, Antipater had unwittingly
saved the life of his own murderer. Cassius and Murcus
assembled an army and gave Herod sole command of it,
making him governor of Coele-Syria with a fleet and a
force of cavalry and infantry. They also promised to make
him king of Judaea after the war which they had just
281   begun against Antony and the young Caesar. Malichus
now became more afraid than ever of Antipater and
proceeded to get rid of him, when they were both dining
with Hyrcanus's cup-bearer, by bribing their host to
poison him. This done,* he used soldiers to keep control
282   of the city; and when Herod and Phasael learned of the
plot against their father, Malichus again met their anger
with denials and disclaimed responsibility for the murder.

283   Such was the death of Antipater, a man distinguished
for his piety and justice and his love of his country. Of his
sons, Herod resolved to avenge his father at once by
leading his army against Malichus, but Phasael, the elder
284   brother, preferred to get the better of the man by cunning,
for fear of appearing to start a civil war. He therefore
accepted Malichus's defence, pretending to believe that he
had had no hand in Antipater's death, and then arranged
a splendid burial for his father. Herod then came to
Samaria, which he found in disorder, but he restored its
fortunes and resolved the disputes among its people.

285   Soon afterwards, when the festival* was held at Jerusalem, he arrived at the city with his soldiers, and Malichus
in alarm urged Hyrcanus to forbid him to enter. Hyrcanus
complied and put forward as the pretext for his exclusion
that it would be wrong to admit a crowd of foreigners
286   during the purification of the people. But Herod disre-
garded his message and entered the city by night, to the
consternation of Malichus, who maintained his pretence
and shed tears for Antipater, making a show of mourning
287   him as a friend. Privately, even so, he provided himself
with a bodyguard. And Herod and his friends decided not
to unmask his hypocrisy, but to allay Malichus's suspicion
by making a friendly response to his gestures.

288   Nevertheless, Herod wrote to Cassius about his father's death, and Cassius, knowing the character of Malichus, wrote in reply that he should avenge his father; and he secretly sent to the military tribunes at Tyre, telling them that Herod had justice on his side and ordering them to
289   assist him. Cassius then captured Laodicea,* where official representatives came to offer him crowns and gifts of money, and Herod expected to settle his account with
290   Malichus when he arrived there. But Malichus, who was near Tyre, in Phoenicia, where his son was a hostage, suspected the truth and conceived a more ambitious design. Coming to the city he determined to rescue his son secretly and to leave for Judaea, and then, when Cassius was preoccupied with attacking Antony, to stir up a national revolt and seize power for himself.

291   But his plans were thwarted by heaven – and by Herod, who was shrewd enough to perceive his purpose. Herod sent ahead a servant, ostensibly to prepare a feast to which he had invited everyone, but in reality to contact the military tribunes and persuade them to come out against
292   Malichus armed with their daggers. And they came out and confronted Malichus on the seashore near the city, where they stabbed the man to death. Hyrcanus was struck dumb with horror at the news, but recovered with some difficulty to enquire of Herod's men what had happened
293   and who had killed Malichus. And when they told him that Cassius had ordered it, he commended their action and declared that Malichus was an utter reprobate who had conspired against his country. This, then, was how Malichus paid the penalty for his crime against Antipater.

294   The departure of Cassius from Syria* was followed by disturbances in Judaea. Helix, who had been left behind in Jerusalem with an army, rose against Phasael, and the
295   people took up arms. Herod was on his way to Fabius, the governor at Damascus, and although he wished to rush to his brother's aid he was prevented by illness. Phasael meanwhile worsted Helix by his own efforts and confined him in a tower, from which he dismissed him under a truce. He also complained of the part played by Hyrcanus, telling him that he had been well served by
296   them and yet was siding with their enemies. It was at that

time that Malichus's brother stirred up a revolt and took control of several fortresses including Masada, the strongest of them all; but Herod, recovered from his illness, moved against him, took from him all the positions he held, and then released him under a truce.

297   Antigonus, the son of Aristobulus, who had raised an army and courted Fabius with bribes, was brought back to Judaea by Ptolemy, the son of Mennaeus, as they were related by marriage.* He had another ally in Marion, installed as prince of Tyre by Cassius – for on occupying Syria, the great man had organised its defence through a

298   system of small princedoms. Marion proceeded to invade Galilee, which lay on his borders, and captured and garrisoned three strongholds, but Herod marched against him and dispossessed him of all his gains. Then, in an act of generosity, he released the Tyrian garrison and even gave

299   some of them gifts, as a gesture of goodwill to their city. This accomplished, he confronted Antigonus, defeated him in battle and drove him out of Judaea, though he had barely set foot across its borders.

On his arrival in Jerusalem Herod was crowned with garlands by Hyrcanus and the people, and he now championed the cause of Hyrcanus all the more after forming a

300   marriage alliance with his family. He had already become engaged to marry the daughter of Alexander,* Aristobulus's son, who was a granddaughter of Hyrcanus, and by whom he was to become the father of three boys and two girls. He had previously married a commoner, a Jewish woman named Doris, the mother of his eldest son Antipater.

Friend of Antony

301   Cassius meanwhile was defeated at Philippi by Antony and Caesar,* as other historians have told. After the victory Caesar made for Italy, while Antony departed for

302   Asia and, on arriving in Bithynia, was met by deputations from every city. Among these were the Jewish leaders, who came to accuse Phasael and Herod of leaving Hyrcanus

303   merely the trappings of kingship* and taking all the power for themselves. Herod, however, who came to defend

himself against his accusers, was highly regarded by
Antony, and in consequence his adversaries were not even
allowed a hearing – a favour which Herod secured from
Antony by a bribe.

304   Antony moved on to Ephesus, and there he received an
embassy sent by the high priest Hyrcanus and our nation,
bringing him a golden crown and requesting him to write
to the provincial governors and set free the Jews taken
captive by Cassius in violation of the laws of warfare, and
305 to restore to them the land taken from them in the time of
Cassius. Antony decided that the Jewish requests were
justified, and wrote at once to Hyrcanus and the Jews. He
also sent decrees to the Tyrians, to the same effect.

306   Marcus Antonius, Imperator, sends greeting to Hyrcanus,
high priest and ethnarch, and to the Jewish nation. I trust
that you are in good health, as I am and my army.

307   Your ambassadors, Lysimachus, son of Pausanias,
Joseph, son of Mennaeus, and Alexander, son of Theodo-
rus, who met me at Ephesus, have renewed the mission
which they formerly discharged at Rome, and have carried
out conscientiously their present mission on behalf of you
308 and your people, making clear your goodwill towards us.
Being convinced, therefore, both by your conduct and by
your words, that you are well disposed to us, and having
regard to your steadfast and god-fearing character, I consider your interests to be my own.

309   When our opponents, enemies of the Roman people,
overran the whole of Asia, sparing neither cities nor temples, in breach of their sworn agreements, it was not only
for ourselves but for all mankind that we fought; and we
took vengeance on them for violating laws both human and
divine. We believe, indeed, that the very sun turned away
310 his light in disgust at the sight of Caesar's foul murder.
Their conspiracy defied the gods themselves, yet Macedonia
made them welcome as if its air were suited to their impious
crimes. At Philippi in that country they got together their
riff-raff of half-crazed malcontents and occupied a natural
fortress walled round by mountains to the sea, the approach
controlled by a single gate. But the gods condemned them
for their wicked enterprise, and we defeated them. Brutus

311 too had escaped to Philippi, where he was trapped by us with the rest of them and shared in Cassius's destruction.

Now that they are punished, it is our hope that hence-forth we shall enjoy peace, and that Asia will have respite
312 from war; and we share with our allies the peace granted us by God, whereby the body of Asia is now healed of the great plague that ravaged it, in consequence of our victory. Having regard, therefore, to your advantage and that of
313 your nation, I shall see that your interests are served. I have sent letters to the cities with instructions that all those persons, whether freemen or slaves, who were sold at auction by Gaius Cassius or his subordinates, shall be set free; and it is my wish that you enjoy the privileges granted by me and Dolabella.* I also forbid the Tyrians to use violence against you, and command that they restore all Jewish property now in their possession. I have accepted the crown that you sent.

314 Marcus Antonius, Imperator, sends greeting to the magistrates, council and people of Tyre.

I have received at Ephesus ambassadors of Hyrcanus, the high priest and ethnarch, who inform me that you are in possession of land which belongs to them, and which you
315 invaded under the regime of our opponents. Since, there-fore, we have undertaken to determine the supremacy by war and, mindful of the cause of piety and justice, have taken vengeance on those who neither remembered kind-nesses nor kept their oaths, it is my wish that our allies shall have peace at your hands. Whatever you received from our adversaries I forbid you to retain: it shall be restored to those from whom it was taken.

316 None of them obtained his province or army by grant of the Senate: they seized them by force, and it was an act of violence to present them to those who served their unlawful
317 ambitions. Now, therefore, that they have paid the penalty, we think it right that our allies should remain in undis-turbed possession of their former territories; and that you should return to Hyrcanus, ethnarch of the Jews, all those places that once were his, and which have come into your possession since the day preceding Cassius's invasion of our province, in pursuit of an unlawful war. And we forbid you

to use any force against them which might render them
incapable of managing their own possessions.

318   If you wish to appeal against him, you may do so on our
arrival in those parts, for we respect the rights of all our
allies equally in giving judgement.

319   Marcus Antonius, Imperator, sends greeting to the magistrates, council and people of Tyre.

I send you herewith my decree, and it is my wish that
you register it in the public tablets, engraved in Roman and
Greek characters, and keep it displayed in full view for
everyone to read.

320   Decree of Marcus Antonius, Imperator, of the triumvirate
appointed to govern the Republic.

Whereas Gaius Cassius, in the recent rebellion, occupied a province to which he had no right, and plundered
it and our allies, and forced the surrender of the Jewish
321   nation, which was a friend of the Roman people: we,
therefore, having overcome his madness by our arms, do
restore by our decrees and judgements the lands plundered by him, that they may be returned to our allies;
and whatever was sold belonging to the Jews, whether
persons or property, shall be released, the persons to their
former freedom and the property to its former owners.

322   It is my wish that whoever disobeys my decree shall
stand trial; and if he be convicted, it shall be my concern
to punish the offender as his conduct merits.

323   He also wrote to the same effect to the people of Sidon,
Antioch and Aradus. We have chosen an appropriate place
to quote these documents, which will provide proof of our
contention that the Romans had our nation's welfare at
heart.

324   After this Antony came into Syria, and while in Cilicia
was visited by Cleopatra, who made him a slave to love.*
Once again he was approached by a hundred of the most
influential Jews, who put forward their most eloquent
speakers to accuse Herod and his brother. Messala spoke
325   in the young men's defence, and Hyrcanus, now Herod's

kinsman by marriage, was present at the hearing, which was held at Daphne.*

After listening to both sides, Antony asked Hyrcanus which of them gave the nation better leadership, and he 326 replied, 'Herod and his brother.' Now Antony had a long-standing friendship with them because of the hospitality he had received from their father while on campaign with Gabinius,* and he now appointed both brothers tetrarchs and entrusted to them the government of the Jews, confirming these arrangements in writing. He also put in chains fifteen of their opponents, and would have killed them but for Herod's intercession.

327 Yet even on their return from this embassy they would not keep quiet, and when Antony decided to stop at Tyre a thousand men went there to meet him. Antony, who had already been heavily bribed by Herod and his brother, ordered the local magistrate to punish the Jewish deputies as revolutionaries, and help to consolidate the power of 328 Herod and his brother. As they stood on the beach before the city, Herod, accompanied by Hyrcanus, hurried out to them and urged them to leave, warning of disaster if they forced the issue. But they refused, and the Romans at once 329 ran out with their daggers, killing some and wounding even more of them, while the rest escaped to their homes and lay low in terror. The incident caused a popular outcry against Herod, and Antony in exasperation killed the men he had taken prisoner.

The Parthians Restore Antigonus

330 Two years later* Syria was seized by Pacorus, son of the king of Parthia, and Barzapharnes, a Parthian satrap. At the same time Ptolemy, the son of Mennaeus, died; and Lysanias, his son, on succeeding to his throne formed a friendly alliance with Antigonus, the son of Aristobulus, with the help of the satrap, who had great influence with 331 Antigonus. Antigonus promised to give the Parthians a thousand talents and five hundred women if they would 332 depose Hyrcanus, transfer his power to himself, and destroy the Herodians; and with this promise, which he did not in fact fulfil, the Parthians marched against Judaea

to restore Antigonus to his country, Pacorus going by the coastal route and Barzapharnes through the interior. The
333 Tyrians shut their gates against Pacorus, but the people of Sidon and Ptolemais admitted him.

Pacorus, however, sent out a troop of cavalry into Judaea to reconnoitre the country and to support Antigo-
334 nus, under the command of the king's cup-bearer and namesake. And when some of the Jews from the neighbourhood of Mount Carmel came over to Antigonus, ready to join in his invasion, he expected with their help to capture part of the country, a place known as Drymi. Their attack was resisted, but his men made their way through to Jerusalem where, their numbers swelled by reinforcements, they came against the palace and laid siege
335 to it. Phasael and Herod came to the relief of the palace, and when battle was joined in the market-place the young men defeated their enemies and pursued them into the Temple precinct. They also posted soldiers in the neighbouring houses to keep them under guard, but they were left without support, and the people rose against them and burned them to death, together with the buildings.

336 Shortly afterwards Herod took vengeance on his opponents for this outrage, engaging them in battle and killing a large number of them.

337 Every day there were skirmishes between them, while the enemy were waiting for the crowds of country-folk
338 who would arrive for the festival called Pentecost; and when the day came, the Temple was surrounded by a great gathering of people, armed and unarmed, numbering many tens of thousands. Their presence secured control of the Temple area, and of the city except for the palace and its precincts, which were defended by Herod with a few
339 soldiers. And now, while Phasael guarded the wall, Herod led out a small company of men to attack the enemy in the suburbs, and after a hard fight, routed them in their tens of thousands, some of them escaping into the city, some to the Temple, and others again to an outer rampart near the walls. Phasael too lent a hand.

340 At the request of Antigonus, Pacorus, the Parthian general, came to the city with a few horsemen, ostensibly to stop the uprising but in reality to assist Antigonus's bid

341 for power. He was met and hospitably received by Phasael, and set a trap for him by advising him to undertake a personal embassy to Barzapharnes; and Phasael, all unsuspecting, acquiesced. Herod, however, condemned the plan, because of the barbarians' treachery, and urged him to set upon Pacorus and his escort.

342 And so Hyrcanus and Phasael set out on their embassy, escorted by Pacorus, who left behind with Herod two hundred cavalry and ten of the so-called Freemen.* When they arrived in Galilee, the enemy who were stationed there came under arms to meet them. Barzapharnes at first

343 welcomed them warmly and gave them gifts, but afterwards began to plot against them.

Phasael and his party were conducted to Ecdippa overlooking the sea; and it was here that they became suspicious of the Parthians, on learning that Antigonus had

344 secured Parthian support against them by his promise of a thousand talents and five hundred women. They were further informed that an armed guard had secretly surrounded them, and that a trap was to be sprung during the night; and they would have been seized, had not the enemy been waiting for the arrest of Herod by the Parthians in Jerusalem, for fear of his escaping at news of their destruction. And the truth of the report was confirmed, when they saw the guards with their own eyes. There were

345 some, therefore, who warned Phasael against further delay and advised him to escape on horseback, and none more urgently than Ophellius, who had heard of their danger from Saramalla, the wealthiest Syrian of his time, and

346 promised him boats for his flight, as they were near the sea. But Phasael had no mind to desert Hyrcanus or endanger his brother, and went to Barzapharnes and denounced the injustice of his plot. If it was money he wanted, he said, he would give him more than Antigonus, and besides, it was an outrage to take the lives of ambassadors who had come to him in trust and did him no

347 wrong. In reply the barbarian swore that there was no truth in his suspicions, and that his fears were groundless; and he then left to join Pacorus.

348 On his departure, some of the Parthians put Hyrcanus and Phasael in chains, while they bitterly reproached the

Parthians for their treachery. Meanwhile the cup-bearer who had been dispatched against Herod had orders to arrest him after luring him outside the city wall. But,

349 fortunately, messengers had been sent by Phasael to expose the Parthian treachery, and on learning that they were apprehended by the enemy, Herod approached Pacorus

350 and the leading Parthians, who had authority over the others. However, although they had full knowledge of the plot, they lied and dissembled, and pressed him to accompany them outside the wall to meet men bearing letters for him; and they insisted that they had not yet been captured by their enemies, and that the men brought news of the

351 success that Phasael had achieved. But Herod had heard from others of his brother's capture, and put no faith in them, and his distrust of the Parthians was deepened through the prompting of Hyrcanus's daughter,* to whose daughter he was betrothed, and who impressed Herod as a highly astute woman, though the others paid no heed to her.

352 The Parthians were reluctant to make an open attempt on a man of Herod's standing, and deferred the matter until the following day while they deliberated what action to take. Herod was now thoroughly alarmed, as he gave more weight to the message about his brother and the Parthian plot than to the other side, and he determined that when evening came he would use the moment to make his escape at once, and entertain no further doubts

353 about the threat from the enemy. So he set out with the soldiers in his command, using beasts of burden to carry the women, that is to say, his own mother and sister, and the daughter of Alexander, son of Aristobulus, his betrothed wife, with her mother, the daughter of Hyrcanus. He also took with him his youngest brother, and all their servants and their company, and followed the

354 road towards Idumaea, unnoticed by the enemy. Yet even among the enemy, there could have been none so hard of heart as to witness their departure without pity for their plight – women weeping and wailing in distress as they led on their little children, abandoning their country and leaving behind their friends in chains, and expecting no better fate themselves.

355   As for Herod himself, however, he raised his spirit above the shock of misfortune and faced the danger with a good courage; and he went along the road urging each of them to take heart and not surrender to despair, which could only hinder their flight, their only hope of safety. And with
356 his encouragement they, for their part, made a new effort to bear their troubles patiently. Yet when a wagon overturned and nearly killed his mother, his anguish on her account, and his fear that the delay caused by the accident would allow the enemy to overtake them, almost drove
357 him to suicide. Indeed, he had drawn his sword and would have dispatched himself, if his companions had not stopped him and overpowered him by their numbers, protesting that he had no right to leave them a prey for the enemy, and that it was ignoble to secure release for himself while regarding his friends' distress with indiffer-
358 ence. Thwarted in his purpose and outnumbered, he felt ashamed at their words and was forced to abandon his reckless attempt on his own life, and instead he revived his mother and had her attended to as well as the urgency of the moment allowed. He then continued on his way, heading for the fortress of Masada with even greater haste. Many were the battles he fought against the Parthians who harassed and pursued him, and he won them all.
359   But his retreat was no more secure from attack by the Jews, who also fell upon them and engaged them hand to hand along the road, when they were sixty stades* from
360 the city. But these too he routed, with a mastery more in keeping with the most thorough preparation and a decisive military advantage than with the grave and desperate position in which he was placed. Later, after he became king, he built a magnificent palace at the place where he defeated the Jews, and round it he founded a city which he named Herodia.
361   On his arrival at a place called Oresa in Idumaea he was met by his brother Joseph, and held a general discussion of their position to decide what must be done. Quite apart from his mercenaries, he had a large following with him, and the fortress of Masada, where he was intending
362 to take refuge, was too small to accommodate such numbers. He therefore dismissed the majority of them, over

nine thousand, and told them to seek safety in various parts of Idumaea, giving them provisions for their journey; while those who were lightly armed and his closest relatives he took with him and reached the fortress. Here he left the women and their escort, who numbered about eight hundred, since they had sufficient grain and water and other necessaries there, and he himself then set out for Petra in Arabia.

363   When day came, the Parthians plundered all the property in Jerusalem, including the palace, and left untouched only the money belonging to Hyrcanus, which amounted
364 to three hundred talents. Much of Herod's property escaped, however, especially as some of it had already been transferred to Idumaea, with a foresight characteristic of the man. And the Parthians, not satisfied with what they found in the city, went out and ravaged the neighbouring countryside as well, reducing the important city of Marisa to ruins.

365   In this way Antigonus was brought back into Judaea by the king of the Parthians, and received Hyrcanus and Phasael as his prisoners; but he was dismayed by the escape of the women, whom he had intended to give to the enemy, together with the money, as their promised
366 reward. And as he was afraid that the people might reinstate Hyrcanus as king, he went up to him where he was held by the Parthian guards and cut off his ears, thereby disqualifying him from the high priesthood for ever; for he was now mutilated, and the law restricts this office to those who are free of physical defects.*

367   As for Phasael, he displayed admirable courage. He realised that he was marked out for slaughter, yet it was not death itself that he dreaded, but to die at the hands of an enemy, which he considered the bitterest and most disgraceful fate. As his hands were chained, therefore, he accomplished his own destruction by dashing his head against a rock, choosing what seemed the most honourable death in such a helpless position, and depriving his enemy
368 of the power to kill him as he pleased. According to one account, however, Antigonus had him killed by privately sending physicians who applied deadly poisons to the
369 gaping wound, under the pretence of treating it. Yet before

Phasael breathed his last he heard from a woman that his brother Herod had escaped the enemy, and he bore his death with a cheerful spirit, survived as he was by one who would avenge his death and had the power to punish his enemies.

King of the Jews

370 Herod, however, was not disheartened by the magnitude of the difficulties that faced him; on the contrary, they made him the more venturesome in the stratagems that he adopted. He now went to Malchus, the Arab king, and recipient of many benefits in the past, in order to obtain a return and in particular to get money, his greatest need, either as a loan or as a gift in recognition of all those that

371 Malchus had received from him. Unaware of what had happened to his brother, he was anxious to ransom him from the enemy, and was prepared to pay them as much as three hundred talents in coin for the price of his redemption; and for the same purpose he took along Phasael's seven-year-old son, to offer him as security to the Arabs.

372 But he was met by messengers from Malchus, by whom the king ordered him to withdraw and declared that the Parthians had forbidden him to receive Herod. This, however, was merely a pretext for not repaying his debts, and he was encouraged in his stand by the leading Arabs, in order to withhold from Herod the monies entrusted to them by

373 Antipater. Herod replied to the messengers that he had come to them with no intention of making trouble, but only to discuss some urgent business of his own.

374 He then resolved to withdraw, and very sensibly took the road to Egypt. The first night he bivouacked in a temple where he had left a large number of his followers, and on the next day came to Rhinocoroura, where he

375 heard the news of his brother's death. Malchus meanwhile regretted his behaviour and hurried after Herod, but to no avail, as Herod was now far away, making haste to reach Pelusium. On arriving, he was refused a passage to Alexandria by ships that lay at anchor there, but he approached the authorities, and respectfully and with great deference

376 they conveyed him to that city. There Cleopatra tried to

detain him, but could not persuade him to stay, as he was too eager to reach Rome, in spite of the winter and reports of serious disturbance and disorder in Italy.

377 And so he set sail from there for Pamphylia,* where he ran into a violent storm and barely reached Rhodes in safety after jettisoning the cargo. He was met here by two
378 of his friends, Sappinus and Ptolemy. He found the city badly damaged from the war against Cassius and, despite his own lack of funds, had no hesitation in giving help, and actually spent beyond his means towards its restoration. He also built a trireme, and putting out from there with his friends made for Italy, and landed at Brundisium.
379 Finally he came to Rome, where he told his story to Antony, beginning with what had befallen him in Judaea. He described how his brother Phasael had been seized and put to death by the Parthians, while Hyrcanus was held prisoner by them; how they had made Antigonus king after he promised them a thousand talents and five hundred women, who were to be from the principal families of the Jewish race; and how he had carried the women out by night and survived many hardships in escaping from
380 the hands of his enemies. And he added that his family, too, were in danger and under siege, and that he had crossed the sea in the depth of winter, and made light of every danger, in his haste to reach Antony, in whom lay all his hopes and his only means of help.
381 Antony was moved to pity by the change in Herod's fortunes, and indulged in the usual reflection concerning men of high rank, that even they are subject to the rule of
382 fortune. He was eager to lend Herod the assistance for which he appealed, for several reasons. He remembered Antipater's hospitality; he had the promise of money from Herod, if he became king, similar to his earlier promise when he was made tetrarch; but above all he hated Antigonus, whom he considered a seditious person and an
383 enemy of the Romans. As for Caesar, he was the more inclined to grant the title and to comply with Herod's wishes because of Antipater's faithful service on his father's campaigns in Egypt,* and his hospitality and unfailing loyalty, quite apart from his desire to oblige Antony in his determined support for Herod's cause.

384   And so Messala, seconded by Atratinus, convened the
Senate, and on presenting Herod to them, gave details of
his father's services and recalled the loyalty that Herod
himself felt towards the Romans; and at the same time
they brought accusations against Antigonus and
denounced him as an enemy, not only for his original
offence against them,* but also for accepting his royal title
385   from the Parthians, in contempt of Rome. The words
angered the Senate, and when Antony stepped forward
and explained to them that it would also be an advantage
in their war against the Parthians if Herod were king, they
agreed unanimously and voted accordingly.

386   Now Herod had not thought that the Romans would
offer him the kingship, as it was their custom to give it to
one of the reigning family; and he had come to the capital
to claim it, not for himself, but for his wife's brother, who
was a grandson of Aristobulus on his father's side and of
387   Hyrcanus on his mother's.* It was therefore the most
striking evidence of Antony's support for Herod that he
not only procured the title for him against his hopes, but
also enabled him to leave Italy with his unexpected gains
388   after a stay of only seven days. Later on, as we shall
describe in its place, Herod put his youthful rival to death.

      When the meeting of the Senate was closed, Antony and
Caesar walked out at Herod's side, preceded by the consuls and the other magistrates, to make sacrifice and to
389   deposit the decree in the Capitol; and Antony gave a
banquet for Herod during the first day of his reign. This,
then, was how Herod became king, having obtained the
title in the hundred and eighty-fourth Olympiad, when the
consuls were Gnaeus Domitius Calvinus, for the second
time, and Caius Asinius Pollio.*

Herod's Advance into Judaea

390   All this time Antigonus was besieging the occupants of
Masada, where, although their other needs were supplied,
there was a shortage of water. Because of this, Herod's
brother Joseph had determined to escape with two hundred of his people and take refuge with the Arabs, as he
had heard that Malchus regretted his discourtesy to

391 Herod. But God stopped him by sending rain in the night;
the cisterns were replenished and escape was unnecessary.
Instead they took new heart, not only because their lack
was made good, but even more because it seemed an act
of God's providence. They sallied out, therefore, and
engaged Antigonus's men, sometimes in open combat and
sometimes by stealth, and they destroyed many of them.

392   Meanwhile Ventidius, the Roman general sent from
Syria to repel the Parthians, first disposed of that enemy
and then turned aside into Judaea, ostensibly to assist
Joseph. But in reality the entire operation was a ploy to
get money from Antigonus, and accordingly he encamped
very close to Jerusalem, and extorted from Antigonus all

393 the money he wanted. Ventidius himself then withdrew
with the bulk of his force, but to prevent his extortion
from being detected, he left behind Silo with a detachment
of soldiers; and Silo too was courted by Antigonus, to
prevent him from damaging his hopes of further assistance
from the Parthians.

394 By this time Herod had sailed from Italy to Ptolemais,
had assembled a considerable army both of foreigners and
of his own countrymen, and was marching through Galilee
against Antigonus. He was supported by Silo and Ventidius, who had been persuaded by Dellius, Antony's emis-

395 sary, to assist in restoring Herod to his country. But
Ventidius was occupied in calming disturbances in the
cities arising from the Parthian occupation, while Silo
remained in Judaea, having been bribed by Antigonus.

As Herod advanced, however, his strength increased by
the day, and the whole of Galilee, with few exceptions,

396 came over to his side. It was essential for him to save the
people besieged in the fortress of Masada, as they were his
relatives; but Joppa, which was in enemy hands, stood in
his way, and had to be captured first, so that the enemy
should be left with no base on his rear as he moved against

397 Jerusalem. Silo now made this his pretext for withdrawing,
and was pursued by the Jews; but although he put up a
feeble defence, he was saved by Herod, who fell upon the
Jews with a handful of his men and routed them. He then
took Joppa and made haste to rescue his relatives in

398 Masada. And now the local people joined his cause, some

because of their affection for his father, others because of Herod's fame, and others again in return for benefits received from both of them; but the majority because of the hopes they entertained at the prospect of a stable monarchy.

399   A formidable army had been assembled, therefore, and as it advanced Antigonus set traps and ambushes at vantage points in the passes, a stratagem that caused virtually
400   no damage to his enemy. After retrieving his relatives from Masada and recapturing the fortress of Oresa, Herod went on to Jerusalem, where he was joined by Silo's army and by many people from the city who were intimidated by his
401   strength. He encamped on the western side of the city, and the guards stationed there assailed his men with javelins
402   and arrows, while others made organised sallies and engaged his front line hand to hand. Herod's first response was to order a proclamation to be made around the walls that he had come for the good of the people and the preservation of the city; and that he would bear no grudge even against his declared enemies, and would grant his bitterest opponents an amnesty for the wrongs done to him.

403   Antigonus replied to Herod's proclamation by telling Silo and the Roman army that they would be in breach of their own principle of justice if they gave the kingship to Herod, who was a commoner and an Idumaean, that is a half-Jew;* and that they ought to offer it to one of the
404   royal family, according to their custom. And he added that even if they were out of sympathy now with him, and had resolved to strip him of the kingship for having accepted it from the Parthians, yet there were many of his family who might lawfully take the title, and would be denied it undeservedly, as they were guiltless of any offence against the Romans, and were priests.

405   The verbal exchange then descended to curses, and Herod allowed his men to defend themselves against their assailants on the wall; and they shot their arrows and easily drove them from the towers in a spirited attack.*

406   It was then that Silo revealed that he had been bribed. He induced a number of his own soldiers to complain aloud about the shortage of provisions, to demand money

for food, and to insist on being taken to suitable quarters for wintering, since Antigonus's soldiers had turned the
407   neighbourhood of the city into a desert. He then began to strike camp and attempted to withdraw. But Herod was insistent in his appeals to Silo's officers and soldiers, urging them not to desert him when he had the backing of Caesar and Antony and of the Senate, and assuring them that he would see them well provided for, and would have the
408   means to supply their needs in abundance. After making this plea he at once set out into the country, and returned with a greater quantity of provisions than anyone had hoped for. He also instructed the people in Samaria who had joined his side to bring to Jericho supplies of every sort, including grain, wine, oil and cattle, to ensure that the soldiers suffered no shortage in the days to come.

409   Antigonus was aware of this activity, and promptly dispatched men across the country to obstruct and ambush them as they collected the food; and in accordance with his orders a large number of armed men gathered near Jericho, and took up position on the hills, keeping watch for the supply column.

410   Nor was Herod idle in the meantime. He took ten cohorts, five Roman and five Jewish, together with mercenaries of various races and a few cavalry, and appeared before Jericho, where he found the city deserted, but captured five hundred men, with their wives and families, occupying the hilltops. He released these prisoners, but the Romans fell upon the city and looted it, finding the houses
411   full of luxuries of every description. Leaving a garrison at Jericho, the king then returned and dismissed the Roman army to their winter quarters* in Idumaea, Galilee and Samaria, the districts which had come over to him. On the
412   other side Antigonus, in requital for his bribe to Silo, succeeded in having part of the army quartered in Lydda, as a sop to Antony. The Romans, then, laid aside their arms and lived off the fat of the land.

413   Herod, however, had no intention of remaining idle, and after sending off his brother Joseph to Idumaea with two thousand foot and four hundred horse, he went to Samaria, where he left his mother and the other relatives who had now quitted Masada, and then proceeded to

414 Galilee to capture some of the strongholds garrisoned by Antigonus. Making his way through to Sepphoris in a snowstorm, he came upon a plentiful supply of provisions there, Antigonus's guards having slipped away.

415 Next, he dispatched a troop of cavalry and three companies of foot-soldiers against some bandits, who were living in caves close to a village called Arbela, and whose
416 depredations he had determined to stop. Forty days later Herod himself arrived with his entire army, and a bold sally by the enemy was forcing back the left wing of his line when he appeared in person with a troop of men, turned their success into a rout, and rallied his faltering
417 troops. Then, as the enemy fled by different routes, he pressed on in pursuit as far as the River Jordan, winning over the whole of Galilee apart from the cave-dwellers. At this point he distributed money to his army, a hundred and fifty drachmas each to the men, and much larger sums to the officers, and then dismissed them to their winter quarters.

418 Meanwhile, he received a visit from Silo and the officers commanding the troops already in winter quarters, as Antigonus was refusing to provide them with food. The man had supplied them for a month and no longer, and had even sent out orders to the people of that region that they should gather in all the produce of the country and make off into the hills, so that the Romans might be
419 destitute and die of starvation. Herod entrusted the care of these men to his youngest brother Pheroras, and ordered him to rebuild Alexandreion also, and Pheroras quickly saw to it that the soldiers had all the supplies that they needed, and restored Alexandreion, which had been left in ruins.

420 About the same time, while Antony was staying in Athens, Ventidius in Syria sent for Silo to join the campaign against the Parthians, but instructed him first to assist Herod in his war, and only afterwards to summon their allies to the war in which the Romans were engaged.
421 Herod, however, who was bearing down on the bandits in the caves, sent Silo off to Ventidius, and struck out against them by himself.

422 The caves were in precipitous hillsides, with their

entrances halfway up the sheer cliffs and surrounded by
rocky crags; it was in such lairs that the bandits lived,
423 with all their dependants. To reach them, the king had
cradles constructed and attached by iron chains to a
winch, by which he lowered them from the hilltop; for the
hill was so steep that his men were unable either to climb
up from below or to slide down against them from above.
424 The cradles were filled with armed men holding long
grappling-hooks, with which they were to seize the bandits
who confronted them and fling them down to their deaths.
The lowering of the cradles proved to be a hazardous
enterprise because of the abyss below, but they held
everything the men needed.
425   When the cradles were let down, none of the men
standing at the mouths of the caves dared to come forward, and they were too afraid to move; but then one of
the soldiers, impatient at the delay caused by their reluctance to engage, buckled on his sword, and grasping with
both hands the chain which held the cradle suspended,
426 lowered himself to the openings of the caves. At one of
these, he first used javelins to drive back most of the men
at the entrance, and then with his grappling-hook dragged
out those who barred his way and thrust them down the
precipice; after which he fell on those inside, slaughtering
many of them, before returning to the cradle and resting.
427 At the sound of their screaming the other cave-dwellers
were gripped by fear and despaired for their lives, but the
whole operation was halted by the onset of night; and
many of them now made overtures with the king's consent
and surrendered themselves into his power.
428   The same method of attack was used on the following
day, with a more sustained assault on them by the soldiers
in the cradles, who fought at their doorways and hurled
firebrands inside; and the caves, which were well stocked
with wood, burst into flames.
429   There was an old man trapped inside with his seven
children and his wife, and when they begged him to let
them slip out to the enemy, he stood at the entrance and
cut down each of his sons as he left, until all were dead,
and then slew his wife. Finally, after hurling their bodies
down the cliff, he threw himself after them, preferring

death to slavery – but not before taunting Herod with his
430 low birth. And yet the king, who had a good view of what
was happening, had held out his right hand and offered
him full immunity. By these means, then, all the caves
were eventually taken.

431   After appointing Ptolemy to take command of that
region, the king left for Samaria with six hundred horsemen and three thousand foot-soldiers to settle accounts
432 with Antigonus. Ptolemy came to grief, however, when the
rebels who had previously caused trouble in Galilee came
out on the attack and took his life; and with this achieved
they took refuge together in the marshes and other inaccessible places, ravaging and plundering the entire district.
433 But Herod returned and punished the insurgents, slaying
some on the spot, and laying siege to those who took
cover in strongholds, before killing them and razing their
fortifications to the ground. And after quelling the rebellion in this way, he also imposed a fine of a hundred
talents on the cities.

434   In the meantime Pacorus had fallen in battle and the
Parthians were routed;* and Ventidius, at Antony's insistence, now sent Machaeras to assist Herod with two legions
435 and a thousand horse. Machaeras, in defiance of Herod's
wishes and at the instigation of Antigonus, by whom he
had been bribed, went off as if to spy out Antigonus's
position. But Antigonus, suspecting his motive in coming
to the city, shut the gates against him, and made plain his
own purpose by checking his approach with sling-shots.
436 Machaeras now realised that Herod's advice had been for
the best, and that he had been mistaken to disregard his
counsel, and he withdrew to the city of Emmaus, slaughtering any Jews he met on the way, friends as well as foes,
437 in his anger at the treatment he had suffered. Indignant at
his behaviour, the king set off for Samaria, determined to
approach Antony about this and inform him that he had
no need of allies who would do more harm to him than to
the enemy, and that he could destroy Antigonus by him-
438 self. Machaeras followed him, begging him to stay, or at
least, if he was resolved to go, to appoint his brother
Joseph to join them in the war against Antigonus; and at
his repeated requests Herod had a change of heart and left

Joseph there with an army, warning him to take no risks and not to quarrel with Machaeras.

439 Herod himself, with horsemen and foot-soldiers who had come to his support, made haste to reach Antony, who was besieging Samosata,* a place near the Euphrates.

440 On arriving at Antioch, he found a large company assembled there who were keen to join Antony, but were deterred from marching out by fear of the barbarians, who were launching attacks along the roads with heavy loss of life. Herod put new heart into these men and undertook to be their leader on the journey.

441 Two days' march from Samosata the barbarians had laid an ambush for men going to join Antony, at a place where the passes leading to the plains were hemmed in by woods. Here they had concealed a large troop of mounted men, whose orders were to keep quiet until their quarry

442 emerged on to the flat ground where they could use their horses. When the men in front came through, the ambush, of about five hundred men, fell upon them suddenly and routed them. But the king, who had been guarding the rear, made for them and by the force of his charge at once drove the enemy back; and his example emboldened his own men, the fugitives rallied to the fight, and the barbar-

443 ians were everywhere cut down. He pressed on with the slaughter until he recovered all their plunder, including many pack-animals and slaves, and then continued on his

444 way. And when the enemy in the woods, near where the pass opened into the plain, attacked them in larger numbers, he engaged these too at the head of a strong body of men and put them to flight with heavy casualties, making the way safe for the rest of the column; and they hailed him as their saviour and protector.

445 When he was close to Samosata Antony sent his army to meet him in full dress uniform, both as a mark of honour to Herod and to lend him support, after hearing

446 of the barbarians' attack on them. He was delighted to see him on his arrival, and on learning of his feats on the way he grasped his hand and spoke warmly of his courage, embracing him and showing special honour to the man he

447 had lately appointed king. Soon afterwards Antiochus surrendered the fortress, and the war came to an end.

Antony then assigned Syria to Sosius, with instructions to assist Herod, and himself departed for Egypt; and Sosius sent ahead two legions into Judaea to reinforce Herod, and followed them with the main body of his army.

448   Now Joseph had already met his death in Judaea, in the following circumstances. Forgetting the warning given him by his brother on his departure to Antony, he had marched quickly to Jericho, with five cohorts lent to him by Machaeras, with the intention of reaping their entire grain

449   harvest, and had pitched camp in the hills. But the Roman army was newly recruited and inexperienced in war, being mostly raised from Syria, and when the enemy attacked there he was caught on unfavourable ground and killed, fighting bravely, with the loss of his whole army; in all, six

450   cohorts were destroyed. Antigonus took possession of the corpses and cut off Joseph's head, although his brother Pheroras offered to redeem it for fifty talents. And after this the Galileans rebelled against the nobility in their country, drowning Herod's partisans in the lake, and much of Idumaea also revolted. Machaeras proceeded to fortify a place called Gittha.

451   Messengers appeared before the king to report these events, and at Daphne near Antioch they informed him of his brother's fate. But Herod was expecting their news – he had had vivid dreams forewarning him of his brother's

452   death. Hurrying on his way, he came to Mount Lebanon, where he added eight hundred of the local men to the Roman legion under his command; and after stopping at Ptolemais he set out by night and advanced through

453   Galilee. The enemy came to meet him, but were defeated in battle and blockaded in the fortress from which they had sallied out the day before. But although he made repeated assaults on it, his efforts were thwarted by a violent storm, and he led his army off to the nearby villages. However, a second legion now arrived from Antony, and the defenders took fright and deserted the fortress during the night.

454   The king now marched at speed to Jericho, determined to take revenge on them for his brother. After finding quarters, he entertained the local magistrates and, when the party was over, said farewell to his guests and went to

455 his room; and what followed is evidence of God's kindness towards the king. The roof of the house collapsed, without killing anyone who was caught inside; and Herod's escaping so great and unexpected a danger convinced everyone that he enjoyed the special favour of God.

456   The next day six thousand of the enemy came down from the hilltops to do battle, but were afraid to engage the Romans.* Their light-armed troops, however, advanced and hurled javelins and stones at the king's men who went out against them, one of them hitting Herod

457 himself in the side with a javelin. Antigonus then sent a general named Pappus to Samaria with a force, to make his enemy believe that he was fighting with men to spare. But while he confronted the general Machaeras, Herod captured five towns, slaughtering the people who were caught in them, about two thousand in number, and burning the towns themselves. He then returned to con-

458 front Pappus, who was encamped near a village called Isana.

      Many people now came pouring out to join him from Jericho and the rest of Judaea. On his approach the enemy advanced boldly to the attack; but he won the engagement, and to avenge his brother pressed hard on them as they fled into the village, and continued the killing. The houses

459 were filled with armed men and many sought refuge on the rooftops, but he overpowered these and tore the roofs from the buildings, exposing the soldiers who were trapped there, huddled together and filling the rooms below. These

460 his men stoned to death from above, piled one upon another; and there was no more terrible sight in all the war than this untold number of bodies lying in heaps between the walls.

461   It was this action above all which broke the spirits of the enemy, as they anxiously awaited the outcome. Large numbers could be seen gathering in the distance around the village, but at this they fled, and only the severity of the weather prevented the king's army in the flush of victory from marching on Jerusalem. There they would have finished the business, as Antigonus was already contemplating headlong flight and the abandonment of the city.

462   It was now late, and the king ordered his soldiers to take their supper, while he went into a room to bathe, feeling exhausted; and it was here that he came in great danger of his life, but by the providence of God escaped.

463   Naked and attended by a single servant he took his bath in the inner chamber, where some of the enemy, who were armed, had been scared into taking refuge. As he bathed, one of them, with drawn sword, slipped out and left by the door, to be followed by a second and a third similarly armed; and in their panic they did the king no harm, and were glad to have got outside unscathed.

464   The next day he cut off the head of Pappus, who had been slain, and sent it to Pheroras in requital for his brother's fate; for it was by the hand of Pappus that he had died.

The Capture of Jerusalem

465   When the storm subsided, he moved from there and came near to Jerusalem,* pitching camp close to the city. It was

466   now the third year since he was proclaimed king at Rome. He then struck camp again and moved close to the wall, at the point where it was most vulnerable to assault, before the Temple. Here he finally made his camp, having decided to attack at the same place as Pompey before him. He fortified this position with three lines of earthworks and erected towers, employing a large gang of men on the

467   work and cutting the available timber. Then, after appointing competent supervisors for these tasks, he left the army still encamped there and went off to Samaria to get married; for, as I have explained earlier, he was betrothed to the daughter of Alexander, son of Aristobulus.

468   After the wedding, Sosius, who had sent his army ahead through the interior, came by way of Phoenicia; and just as the general appeared with a large army of horse and foot, the king also arrived from Samaria bringing about thirty thousand men, a substantial reinforcement to his

469   army. They joined forces before the wall of Jerusalem and were deployed near the north wall of the city, an army consisting in all of eleven battalions of infantry and six

thousand cavalry, as well as auxiliaries from Syria. Their
two commanders were Sosius, sent to provide support by
Antony, and Herod, pursuing his personal aim of wresting
power from Antigonus, who was declared an enemy at
Rome, and taking his place as king, in accordance with
the Senate's decree.

470   The entire Jewish nation being confined together within
the walls, they organised their resistance to Herod and his
army with fanatical zeal. Many prophecies were uttered
around the Temple, and much was said to reassure the
people that God would deliver them from their dangers.

471   From outside the city they carried off whatever might
serve as sustenance for men or beasts, and they sent out
raiding parties under cover to cut off their supplies. When

472   Herod saw this, he countered their raids by posting
ambushes at strategic points, and sent companies of foot-
soldiers to gather supplies from a distance, so that they

473   soon had plenty of provisions. The raising of the three
lines of earthworks had also been accomplished smoothly,
with many hands continuously employed on them; for it
was summer, and their construction suffered no hindrance
either from the weather or from the workforce.

They now brought up their artillery and began to batter
474   down the wall, using every resource. The defenders, however, were not cowed, and opposed these tactics with
various stratagems of their own. They would dash out and
set fire to their constructions, whether completed or half-
finished; and when they engaged them hand to hand they
were a match for the Romans in bravery, though inferior

475   in skill. Against the artillery they built new defences as the
first ones collapsed, and they went underground to meet
the enemy and fought them in the mines. And so, more
from desperation than from rational foresight, they persisted in the struggle to the very last – and this despite
being surrounded by a mighty army and, as it was a
sabbatical year,* suffering starvation through their lack of
provisions.

476   The first to scale the wall were twenty picked men,
followed by the centurions of Sosius; and the first wall
was taken in forty days, the second in fifteen. Some of the
porticoes around the Temple were set on fire, an act for

which Herod held Antigonus responsible and thereby con-
477 trived to draw the hatred of the Jews upon him. After the
capture of the outer precincts of the Temple and the Lower
City, the Jews sought refuge in the inner precincts and the
Upper City; and fearing that the Romans would prevent
them from offering their daily sacrifices to God, they sent
ambassadors to request a single concession – that sacrifi-
cial victims might be brought in for them. Herod agreed
478 to this, assuming that they would surrender. But when he
saw that his expectations were vain, and that they were
persisting in their stubborn defence of Antigonus's title, he
attacked and took the city by storm.

479   A wholesale massacre now followed, in every quarter of
the city, as the Romans were enraged at the length of the
siege, while Herod's Jewish allies were anxious that no
480 opposition should survive. They were slaughtered indis-
criminately, whether crushed together in the narrow streets
and houses or seeking refuge at the Sanctuary, and there
was no pity shown to infants or old age and no mercy for
the frailty of women. Even though the king sent word
around and urged them to forbear, no one stayed his
hand, but they fell upon their victims like madmen, mak-
481 ing no distinction of age. It was then that Antigonus,
heedless of both his past and present fortunes, came down
from the citadel and fell at Sosius's feet; but Sosius, with
no pity for his change of fortune, broke into unrestrained
applause, and dubbed him 'Antigone'.* He did not, however, treat him like a woman and let him go unguarded,
but put him in chains and held him in close custody.

482   Herod's concern, once in control of his enemies, was to
control his many foreign allies, who were bent on getting
483 a sight of the Temple and the sacred contents of the
Sanctuary. He kept them back by appeals or threats, and
in some cases even by force of arms, believing that victory
would be a harder fate than defeat, if such people should
484 see what was forbidden to men's eyes. He also tried to
prevent the pillage of the city by protesting to Sosius, that,
if the Romans emptied the city of its money and men, they
would leave him king of a wilderness, and that he would
consider even the dominion of the whole world a poor
485 recompense for the slaughter of so many citizens. Sosius

replied that he had a right to permit his soldiers to pillage, as their reward for the siege; and at this the king said that
486 he would pay each one of them from his private funds, and so redeemed the city from further destruction. And he fulfilled his promise, rewarding each soldier handsomely and their officers in proportion, and showing a truly royal generosity to Sosius himself, so that they were all much the wealthier on their departure.

487 This disaster befell the city of Jerusalem in the consulship at Rome of Marcus Agrippa and Caninius Gallus,* in the hundred and eighty-fifth Olympiad,* in the third month, on the day of the Fast.* It was like a repetition of the misfortune that the Jews had suffered in the time of
488 Pompey, as they were captured by Sosius on the very same day, after an interval of twenty-seven years.

After dedicating a golden crown to God, Sosius moved his army from Jerusalem, and took Antigonus in chains to
489 Antony. But Herod was apprehensive that if Antigonus were kept in custody and taken to Rome by Antony, he might plead his cause before the Senate, adducing his own descent from kings and Herod's common birth, and argu-
490 ing that the royal title belonged to his sons by virtue of their lineage, whatever his own offence against the Romans. Prompted by such anxiety, Herod persuaded Antony with a large bribe to put Antigonus to death. And this was done,* at once releasing Herod from his fear and bringing to an end the rule of the Hasmonaean line, after a hundred and twenty-six years. They were an illustrious dynasty, distinguished by their lineage and their priestly
491 office, and by the services rendered to the nation by their founders; but their feuding with one another lost them their power, and it passed to Herod, son of Antipater, a man of common birth and from a private household, the subjects of kings. This, then, is the account we have received of the end of the Hasmonaean line.

BOOK XV

The Opposition Purged

1 We have shown in the previous book how Sosius and
Herod took Jerusalem by storm, and also made a prisoner
of Antigonus, and we shall now describe the sequel to
those events.

2 After assuming control over the whole of Judaea, Herod
gave honoured positions to those people in the city who
had supported his cause when he was still a commoner, but
never let a day pass without punishing and taking revenge
3 on the allies of his enemies. Pollion the Pharisee and his
disciple Samaias were particularly honoured by him,
because during the siege of Jerusalem they advised the
citizens to admit Herod; and for this they received their due
4 reward. It was this same Pollion, when Herod was on trial
for his life, who had reproached Hyrcanus and the judges
and forewarned them that, if Herod were spared, he would
one day turn on them all;* and in time this came to pass,
and God brought his words to fulfilment.

5 But at the time of his capture of Jerusalem, Herod collected
all the valuables in his kingdom, robbing the wealthy classes
in the process, and used all the silver and gold that he
acquired to make gifts to Antony and his friends. He also
6 killed forty-five leading members of Antigonus's party, and
to prevent anything being carried out with the dead he
stationed guards at the city gates, who searched the corpses
and brought back to the king whatever silver or gold or
other valuables they found on them. There was no end to
7 their miseries, plundered as they were by the greed of their
impecunious master, and yet forced to leave the land untill-
led in the sabbatical year which was then upon them; for in
that year we are forbidden to sow the earth.*

8 After receiving Antigonus as his captive, Antony decided

to keep him in chains until his triumph,* but when he heard
that the nation were becoming seditious, and were still
loyal to Antigonus out of hatred for Herod, he determined
to behead him at Antioch, as the Jews could hardly be kept
9 quiet otherwise. My account is confirmed by the following
words of Strabo of Cappadocia: 'Antigonus the Jew was
brought to Antioch, where Antony beheaded him. He was
the first Roman who condemned a king to be beheaded,
believing that there was no other way to win over the Jews
to accept Herod, who had been appointed in his place.
Even under torture, they would not submit to proclaiming
him king, so great was their regard for their former king.
10 He supposed, therefore, that this dishonourable death
would somewhat diminish the respect with which they
remembered Antigonus, and also lessen their hatred of
Herod.' Such is Strabo's account.
11   After Herod had secured the kingship, the news reached
Hyrcanus the high priest, who was held captive by the
Parthians; and he was released from captivity and came to
12 Herod. This came about as follows. Barzapharnes and
Pacorus, the Parthian generals, captured Hyrcanus, who
had been appointed at first high priest and then king,
together with Herod's brother Phasael, and took them off
13 to Parthia. But Phasael could not endure the disgrace of
imprisonment and, believing that death with honour was
better than life at any cost, he contrived his own death, as I
described earlier.
14   However, when Hyrcanus was brought before him,
Phraates, the Parthian king, dealt very kindly with him; for
he was already apprised of his distinguished and noble
lineage, and on this account released him from his bonds
and permitted him to settle in Babylon, where there was a
15 large Jewish population. These people honoured Hyrcanus
as their high priest and king, as did all the Jewish nation
who inhabited that region as far as the Euphrates; and he
was gratified by their regard for him.
16   But when he learned that Herod had become king, he
began to entertain new hopes, since he had always held him
in affection and expected also that Herod would recall the
favour he had done him in protecting him from the danger
of punishment, when he was put on trial and facing the

death sentence. And so, eager to go to Herod, he discussed
17 his intention with the Jews. But they tried to keep him
there, begging him to remain and reminding him that from
them he enjoyed in full the good offices and honours due to
high priests and kings, and, what was still more important,
that he was debarred from these honours in Judaea because
of the disfigurement inflicted on him by Antigonus. They
also put it to him that favours which men have received as
commoners are not repaid in like manner when they
become kings, since they change quite naturally with their
change of fortune.

18   Such were the inducements that they offered Hyrcanus,
but his desire to get away was unshaken. A letter now
arrived from Herod, requesting Hyrcanus to ask Phraates
and the Jews of that region not to resent the fact that he
would be sharing the kingship with Herod, as the time was
now ripe for a return of the kindness Hyrcanus had showed
19 him both in his nurture and in saving his life. As well as this
letter to Hyrcanus, he also sent his envoy Saramalla with a
generous number of gifts to Phraates, to persuade him not
to prevent his requiting his benefactor with the same kind-
20 ness that he had received. It was not this, however, that was
the source of his concern, but the fact that he himself had
no legitimate title to the kingship, and so had good grounds
to fear a reversal; and his real concern was to have Hyrcanus in his power, or even to get rid of him altogether, as
he later did.

21   Hyrcanus for his part allowed himself to be persuaded,
and returned to Judaea with the consent of the Parthian
king and the financial support of the Jews.

On the occasion of his arrival, however, Herod received
him with every mark of respect, and assigned him the first
place at councils and the seat of honour at banquets, and
called him father; and by these and other means he kept
him deceived, and contrived to pursue his treacherous
design without causing suspicion.

The Murder of Aristobulus

22 He also tried to consolidate his power by other calculated
moves which only resulted in dissension within his own

household. He was wary, for example, of appointing a well-known figure to be the high priest of God, and so summoned from Babylon a somewhat obscure priest named Ananel, and gave the high priesthood to him.

23   The insult was at once resented by Alexandra, daughter of Hyrcanus and wife of King Aristobulus's son, Alexander.* She had two children by Alexander, a son called Aristobulus, an extremely handsome youth, and Herod's wife Mariamme, also conspicuous for her beauty; and she

24   was deeply aggrieved at this dishonour to her son, that while he was still alive an outsider should be preferred to the office of high priest. She therefore wrote to Cleopatra, and asked her to intercede with Antony and obtain the high priesthood for her son, and the letter was delivered with the help of a professional musician.

25   Antony was slow to respond, but his friend Dellius came to Judaea on some business, and when he saw Aristobulus was deeply affected by his charm and marvelled at the boy's stature and beauty; and the king's wife, Mariamme, made no less an impression on him. And so assured was

26   he of the beauty of Alexandra's children that, when their mother came to speak with him, he urged her to have both their portraits painted and sent to Antony, telling her that once he had seen them he would grant any request she

27   might make. Delighted by the suggestion, Alexandra sent the portraits to Antony accompanied by some extravagant praise from Dellius, to the effect that they resembled the children of a god rather than of human parents. But Dellius had a purpose of his own in saying this, which was to tempt Antony into having his pleasure with them.

28   Antony, however, was embarrassed to send for the girl, as she was married to Herod, and he was too conscious of the gossip that would reach the ears of Cleopatra if he did so. He therefore gave orders that the boy should be sent, and with a show of respectability added 'provided it is no

29   trouble'. When this was reported to Herod, he judged it unsafe to send Aristobulus to Antony, in view of the exceptional beauty of the boy, who was just sixteen, and of his noble birth; for Antony was more powerful than any Roman of his time, was ready to make him his lover, and was enabled by his power to indulge his pleasures

30 without reserve. Accordingly he wrote in reply that the boy's departure would be enough on its own to plunge the whole country into civil war, as the Jews had formed hopes of overthrowing the government and installing a new king.

31 After making these excuses to Antony, he decided not to leave the boy and Alexandra entirely without honour, as his wife Mariamme was urging him persistently to restore the high priesthood to her brother, and he also judged it to be in his own interests; for Aristobulus would be unable to leave the country once the office was conferred on him. He therefore called a council of his friends, and bitterly accused Alexandra of having secretly plotted

32 against his royal authority, and of scheming through contact with Cleopatra to get Antony to remove him from power, and allow the youth to take over as head of state.

33 But Alexandra had been wrong, he argued, to form such a design, since her own daughter would also be deprived of the dignity she now had, and her plot would mean the disruption of the kingdom which he had won with such difficulty and in the face of no ordinary dangers. Neverthe-

34 less, he said, he would forget her misconduct and continue to deal justly with them; and he was now prepared to give her son the high priesthood, to which he had formerly

35 appointed Ananel only because of Aristobulus's extreme youth. These words of Herod's were not idly spoken but after careful deliberation, in order to deceive the women and his friends who were gathered there.

Alexandra was overcome with emotion, at once delighted by his unexpected offer and frightened by the

36 suspicion she was under, and she began her defence in tears. As to the high priesthood, she admitted having made every possible effort to procure it for her son, because of the dishonour to him; but she had no designs on the royal power, and would not accept it if it came her way – she had honour enough as it was, because of Herod's power and the security which all her family enjoyed through his unrivalled talent for government. For the present, she

37 declared herself overcome by his generosity and ready to accept the honour for her son, and to give Herod her unqualified obedience. And she asked his pardon if, by

reason of her royal birth and her customary frankness, she had allowed her sense of injustice to cause her to act

38 overhastily. After such an exchange of words, and earnest and protracted assurances of their good faith, they parted with all suspicion apparently allayed.

39 And so King Herod at once took the high priesthood away from Ananel, who, as we said before, was not a native of Judaea but descended from the Jews who were taken into captivity beyond the Euphrates. There were many tens of thousands of this people who had been

40 transported and were living in Babylonia, and it was from there that Ananel came, a man of high-priestly family and an old and close friend of Herod. But just as Herod had honoured him, on becoming king, so he now dismissed him to put an end to his domestic troubles. In this, however, he acted unlawfully, for no one had ever been lawfully deprived of this office when once he had assumed

41 it. Antiochus Epiphanes* was the first to break the law by dismissing Jesus and appointing his brother Onias; the next was Aristobulus, who dismissed his brother Hyrcanus;* and Herod became the third when he transferred the dignity to the young Aristobulus.

42 For the moment, Herod seemed to have healed his domestic disputes, but as was natural after a reconciliation, he did not remain free of suspicion; for Alexandra's past attempts gave him reason to fear that, if she found an opportunity, she would try to overthrow him. He therefore

43 instructed her to remain in the palace and to do nothing without his authority, and she was kept under close watch, so that not even the routine activities of her daily life escaped his notice.

44 All this gradually turned her wild with anger, and hatred began to grow within her. She was full of a woman's pride and resented the surveillance that his suspicions required, and she thought that anything would be better than to live out her life in a state of slavery and fear, deprived of her

45 liberty of speech and with only the semblance of honour. And so she wrote to Cleopatra, making a long complaint of her circumstances and entreating her to give her all the help she could. Cleopatra told her to escape secretly with

46 her son and come to her in Egypt, and she accepted the

advice and contrived the following scheme. She had two coffins made, as if for the removal of the dead, and put herself and her son inside them; and she had ordered some servants whom she had acquainted with the plan to bear them out by night. From there a road would lead them to the sea, where there was a ship prepared for them to sail to Egypt.

47 However, her servant Aesop thoughtlessly mentioned these preparations to Sabbion, one of her friends, supposing that he knew of the plan. Now Sabbion had previously been an enemy of Herod, because he was suspected of involvement in the plot to poison Antipater, but he now saw his chance to turn Herod's hatred into friendship by giving him the information he had learned; and so he
48 revealed Alexandra's plot to the king. Herod allowed her to proceed to the execution of her project, and then caught her in the very act of escaping. He overlooked her offence, however, not daring to deal harshly with her, though he would gladly have done so, as he believed that Cleopatra – who hated Herod – would not have tolerated his accusing her; and he made a show of magnanimity, as if his
49 pardoning them were simply an act of generosity. He was determined, however, to get rid of the young man by one means or another, but thought that he would be more likely to avoid detection if he refrained from acting immediately after what had happened.

50 The feast of Tabernacles now began,* which is one of the most important festivals that we observe, and Herod, biding his time, spent these days in rejoicing with the rest of the people. Yet even from celebrations such as these he was clearly stung by envy, and provoked to a swifter
51 execution of his purpose. Aristobulus was a youth of seventeen, and when he went up to the altar to offer the sacrifices according to the law, wearing the vestments of the high priest and performing the solemn rites, he was extraordinarily handsome and taller than his years, the beauty of his features a perfect testimony to the nobility
52 of his descent. The people felt a surge of affection for him, and the vivid memory of his grandfather Aristobulus's deeds came to their minds; and they gradually revealed the feelings that overpowered them, uneasy even while they

celebrated, calling out their good wishes to him along with
their prayers. The affection in which the crowds held him
was not in doubt, but their acknowledgement of their
emotions seemed somewhat rash in a people ruled by a
king.

53   The whole episode made Herod resolve to carry through
his design against the boy. When the festival was over, he
was being entertained at Jericho, where Alexandra had
invited them, and he befriended the boy and led him on to
drink without a care, and was ready to join in his sport

54 and act like a youngster to honour him. But as the place
was peculiarly hot, the guests soon went out together for
a stroll, and they stood beside the large swimming-pools
adjacent to the palace, cooling themselves from the burn-

55 ing heat of noon. At first they watched some of Herod's
servants and friends swimming, and then, at Herod's
insistence, the boy was induced to join them. It was now
getting dark, and as he swam some of the friends, obeying
their instructions, kept pushing him down and holding

56 him underwater as if in sport; but they did not stop until
they had finally drowned him. Such was the manner of
Aristobulus's murder, when he was not yet eighteen years
of age. And the high priesthood, which he had held for a
year, was regained by Ananel.

Alexandra's Intrigues Against Herod

57 When the grave news reached the women, their joy was at
once changed to lamentation and ungovernable sorrow at
the sight of the dead body that was laid before them; and
as the word was spread abroad, the whole city of Jerusalem was deeply grieved, every family feeling the misfortune

58 as its own. Alexandra was especially distraught as she
realised the truth about her son's death, but although her
knowledge of how it was accomplished made her grief the
more bitter, she felt constrained to bear up bravely for fear

59 of compounding the evil. There were many times when
she came close to ending her life by her own hand, yet she
refrained, in the hope that if she lived she might avenge
her son's treacherous and unlawful killing. It was this
hope that strengthened her will to live, and the thought

that, by giving no hint of her suspicion that her son's death was premeditated, she would be assured of an
60 opportunity for revenge. She remained resolute, therefore, in concealing her suspicion.

And Herod, for his part, convincingly dispelled any suspicion in the public at large that the boy's death had been premeditated, not merely by the customary signs of mourning, but by a tearful and unfeigned display of the turmoil in his heart. Indeed, it may well be that his emotions overcame him at the sight of the boy's youthful beauty, even though he had considered his death essential to his own security, and for all that his present actions were calculated to disclaim responsibility. And certainly
61 he lavished every expense on his funeral, providing a splendid tomb and a profusion of spices, and burying a large number of ornaments with the body; and to this extent he took away some of the bitterness from the women's grief and brought them some consolation.

62 Alexandra, however, was not won over by such gestures, and her painful memory of the crime made her increasingly querulous and resentful; and so she wrote to Cleopatra about Herod's plot and the murder of her son.
63 Cleopatra was already anxious to respond to Alexandra's pleas for help, out of pity for her ill fortune, and she now made the whole business her personal concern, repeatedly urging Antony to avenge the boy's murder. It was not right, she insisted, that Herod, who had no claim to the kingship which Antony had conferred on him, should
64 display such lawlessness towards those of royal blood. Persuaded by this, Antony, on his departure for Laodicea,* wrote to Herod and ordered him to come there and clear himself of the charges concerning Aristobulus, saying that he regarded the plot, if it was of Herod's devising, as a criminal act.

65 The accusation frightened Herod, as did the enmity of Cleopatra, who had worked unremittingly to turn Antony against him. He therefore decided to obey, as no other course lay open to him, and left his uncle Joseph in charge of the government of the country, with secret instructions that, if anything happened to him while he was with Antony, he should at once do away with Mariamme as

66 well. He gave as his reason the great love he felt for his
wife and his fear of the insult to his name, even after his
death, if her beauty should make her the object of another
67 man's affections – this being no more than an intimation
of Antony's desire for the woman, of whose beauty he had
already heard tell. And so, with these instructions, Herod
went away to meet Antony, his whole future lying in the
balance.

68   Now that Joseph was in charge of the kingdom's affairs,
he regularly had meetings with Mariamme, whether about
matters of public business or as a mark of the respect
which he owed her as his queen, and he frequently fell to
telling of Herod's kindness and deep love for her. Mar-
69 iamme, and Alexandra even more, affected with womanly
banter to disbelieve his words, and in an excess of zeal to
demonstrate the king's feelings Joseph was drawn into
disclosing his instructions, as a sure proof that Herod
could not live without her, and that if he suffered an ill
70 fate he could not endure to be parted from her even in
death. This was Joseph's assurance; but the women naturally seized on his words as evidence, not of Herod's
deep feeling of love, but rather of his cruelty, inasmuch as
not even his death would save them from destruction by
the fiat of the tyrant. It was a cruel inference, therefore,
that they drew from what they had been told.

71   At this time the word went round the city of Jerusalem
that Antony had tortured Herod and put him to death.
This rumour, which was originated by Herod's enemies,
naturally startled everyone in the palace, and especially
72 the women. Alexandra tried to persuade Joseph to leave
the palace with them and seek refuge with the standards
of the Roman legion, which was then encamped about the
city, under the command of Julius, to protect the king's
73 position. She argued that by doing so they would win the
friendship of the Romans and enjoy greater security, if any
disturbance occurred in the palace; and further, that she
had hopes of realising her whole ambition if Antony
should set eyes on Mariamme, since he would be their
means of recovering the kingdom and obtaining everything
to which their royal birth gave them title.

74   While they were occupied with these deliberations, they

received a letter from Herod, giving an account of his whole position which contradicted the rumour that had
75 circulated earlier. According to this, when he came before Antony, he had quickly won him over with the gifts he had brought from Jerusalem, and in conversation had promptly dispelled Antony's displeasure with him. Cleopatra's arguments had had little force in comparison with
76 Herod's way of gaining favour. Antony had said that it was wrong to require a king to give an account of his reign, since at that rate he would be no king at all, and that those who had given him his title and conferred authority upon him should allow him to exercise it. And to the same purpose he had told Cleopatra that it would be better for her not to meddle in the conduct of the king's government.
77   This was the content of Herod's letter, in which he also enlarged upon the other honours he received from Antony, such as sitting with him when he gave judgement and dining with him every day, favours that he enjoyed in spite of Cleopatra's bitter charges against him; for she coveted his land, and was demanding his kingdom for herself and anxiously exploring every means of getting rid of him.
78 Antony, however, he found to be fair-minded, and he was no longer apprehensive of harsh treatment at his hands; on the contrary, he said, he would very soon return home with the advantage of having strengthened Antony's
79 goodwill towards his kingship and his government. As for Cleopatra, she had no hope of further aggrandisement, since Antony had given her Coele-Syria instead of the land she desired, and by this means had at once appeased her and unburdened himself of her persistent pleas for Judaea.
80   When this letter was brought, the women abandoned the project of taking refuge with the Romans, which they had formed on the assumption that Herod was dead. Their intention, however, did not remain a secret, for when the king returned to Judaea after escorting Antony on his way to attack the Parthians, his sister Salome and his mother revealed the purpose that Alexandra and her friends had
81 entertained. Salome also slandered her husband Joseph by claiming that he was carrying on an adulterous relationship with Mariamme, her motive for saying this being her

long-standing hatred of the other woman, who took a haughty attitude in their quarrels and reproached her family with their low birth.

82   Herod, deeply shaken by her words, was unable to bear his jealousy, such was the warmth and intensity of his love for Mariamme; yet he kept sufficient hold of himself to refrain from any hasty act of passion, and questioned Mariamme in private about the allegations concerning

83   Joseph, his devotion and his jealousy combining to torment him. When she denied the charge on oath, and said everything in her defence that an innocent woman could say, the king eventually accepted her story, his temper softened, and yielding to the love he felt for his wife, he went so far as to apologise for giving the impression that

84   he believed what he had heard. He went on to acknowledge his great gratitude for the propriety of her behaviour, and assured her of the strength of his love and affection for her; until at last, as is usual between lovers, they fell to weeping, and embraced one another with deep emotion.

85   But as the king continued to give pledges of his feeling for her, Mariamme said, 'It was not the act of a lover to command that, if he came to any harm at the hands of

86   Antony, I too should be put to death, though guiltless of any fault.' When these words escaped her lips, the king became distraught and at once pushed her from his embrace; and he tore his hair, and shouted that he now had the clearest proof of Joseph's intimacy with her – he

87   would not have disclosed his secret unless they enjoyed each other's complete confidence.

In the state he was in he came close to killing his wife, but his love for her prevailed and he resisted the impulse, though barely restraining himself in his anguish. Joseph, however, he ordered to be put to death without even admitting him into his sight, and he held Alexandra in chains and under custody as an accomplice in all this mischief.

Herod and Cleopatra

88   Meanwhile Syria was in disorder. Cleopatra was unrelenting in her efforts to persuade Antony to attack all its

rulers, and deprive them of their several dominions and give them to her; and she had great influence over him by reason of the desire he felt for her. Covetous by nature, she

89 stopped at no act of wickedness. She had known that her brother* stood to inherit her kingdom and had prevented his succession by poisoning him at the age of fifteen; and she had had her sister Arsinoe killed by Antony when she was a suppliant at the temple of Artemis at Ephesus.

90 Wherever she had the merest hope of getting wealth she desecrated both temples and sepulchres: no shrine was deemed too hallowed to be stripped of its ornaments, and any public place that might satisfy the greed of this unscrupulous woman would be plundered with criminal

91 abandon. In short, nothing could bring her contentment, extravagant as she was and enslaved to her appetites, and everything fell short of the ambitions she entertained.

It was for this reason that she was continually urging Antony to dispossess others of their dominions and give them to her, just as now, after travelling through Syria with him, she was contriving to get possession of that

92 country. To this end, she accused Lysanias,* the son of Ptolemy, of inviting the Parthians to interfere in its affairs, and had him put to death; and she asked Antony for Judaea and Arabia, requesting the removal of their kings.

93 Antony, it was true, was so totally dominated by the woman that he seemed to obey her every wish not only because of their intimacy but like a man under the spell of drugs; yet the obvious injustice of it made him ashamed to acquiesce in her most outrageous demands. In order,

94 therefore, not to deny her altogether, nor to appear patently in the wrong by carrying out everything she required, he took away some parts of either king's territory

95 and presented them to her. He also gave her the cities between the river Eleutherus and Egypt, but made an exception of Tyre and Sidon, in spite of her importunate appeals that they should be included in his gift, as he knew that they had been free cities from the time of their ancestors.

96 After gaining possession of these lands, Cleopatra accompanied Antony on his campaign against Armenia as far as the Euphrates, and then turned back and visited Apamea

and Damascus before continuing into Judaea. Here she was met by Herod, who leased from her the parts of Arabia given to her by Antony and the revenues due to her from the region of Jericho; and this is the land where balsam grows, the most precious of its products and unique to those parts, and also an abundance of fine date-palms.

97   During these transactions she became more intimate with Herod and attempted to seduce the king. It was never her nature to disguise her enjoyment of such pleasures, and she may in fact have felt some passion for him; or else, more probably, she secretly intended by his violation of her to lay a trap for him. In short, she gave every appearance of being overcome by desire.

98   Herod, however, was never well disposed towards Cleopatra, knowing her to be invariably a cause of trouble, and he now had reason to despise her, if it was lust that made her so forward, while if treachery were the motive for her advances he was resolved to forestall her and get his revenge. He therefore rejected her overtures, and suggested to his friends the idea of killing her while he had her in his power, arguing that the many wrongs suffered

99   or anticipated by the victims of her cruelty would thereby be cancelled, and that her death would also benefit Antony, since she would not prove faithful even to him if he were ever forced to require her loyalty in time of need.

100   But his friends discouraged the plan, telling him in the first place that it would be a mistake to overreach himself and expose himself to such obvious danger, and urgently

101   entreating him not to act in haste. Antony, they said, would not condone it, however forcefully the advantage might be represented to him, as his love would be the more inflamed by the thought that he had lost her through violence and treachery; while no adequate justification could be found for an attempt against a woman of higher standing than any of her contemporaries. And as to any supposed benefit, that would be plainly compromised by

102   his reckless disregard for Antony's feelings. From these considerations it was not hard to see that Herod's reign and his family would suffer serious and lasting damage, when it was in his power to avoid the offence into which she was tempting him and settle the issue with dignity.

103   Such representations of the likely risk made him afraid, and caused him to abandon the undertaking; and he courted Cleopatra with gifts and escorted her towards Egypt.

104   After Antony had taken Armenia, he sent Artabazes, the son of Tigranes, as a prisoner to Egypt, together with his sons and satraps, and made a present of them, and of all the valuables that he had taken from the kingdom, to

105   Cleopatra. Artaxias, the eldest son of Artabazes, who had escaped on that occasion, became king of Armenia, but was deposed by Archelaus and Nero Caesar, who restored his younger brother Tigranes to the throne. But these things happened later.

106   As for the tribute which he had to pay for the land given to Cleopatra by Antony, Herod dealt fairly with her, since he thought it would be unsafe to give Cleopatra any reason

107   to hate him. The king of Arabia, on the other hand, whose tribute Herod had assumed responsibility for collecting, sent him the two hundred talents for a time but then became uncooperative and slow in making the payments; and if only a part of his dues were wrung from him, even then he was unwilling to hand it over without some deduction.

War with the Nabataean Arabs

108   Because of the Arab's unscrupulous dealing, which finally took the form of a complete refusal to honour his obligations, Herod was set to march against him, but gave

109   priority to the Roman war. The Battle of Actium was now imminent,* which took place in the hundred and seventy-eighth Olympiad, and in which Caesar was to contest with Antony the dominion of the world. Herod, whose land had been yielding rich harvests for a long time and who had revenues and resources at his disposal, recruited an army to assist Antony, fully equipped to the last detail.

110   Antony, however, said that he had no need of his help, and ordered him to march against the Arab, of whose untrustworthiness he had learned from both Herod and Cleopatra. It was in fact at Cleopatra's request that he gave this order, as she thought it would be to her

advantage if one of the kings suffered a reverse at the hands of the other.

111   On receiving this message from Antony, Herod turned back and kept his army together with the intention of invading Arabia immediately; and with a force of cavalry and infantry prepared he came to the city of Dion. Here the Arabs, who were aware of his preparations for war, came to meet him, and in a fierce battle the Jews were victorious.

112   Afterwards, however, a large army of Arabs assembled at Canata, a place in Coele-Syria, and Herod, who had prior intelligence of their movements, came to meet them with most of his force. On approaching, he decided to pitch camp on favourable ground and to put up a palisade,

113   so as to attack from a position of vantage; but as he was making these dispositions, the Jews all began shouting for him to put an end to the delay and lead them against the Arabs. They were encouraged by their confidence in being well organised, and the most eager of them all were those who had won the first battle and had given the enemy no

114   chance to fight hand to hand. And so, because of their clamour and the great enthusiasm they displayed, the king decided to exploit his army's readiness. Promising that he would not fail to match their valour, he armed himself and led the attack, while they all followed in their own companies.

115   Panic at once seized the Arabs, who after a brief resistance saw that the Jews were invincible and full of spirit, and most of them gave way and began to flee. And they

116   would have been wiped out, if Herod and the Jews had not been worsted by Athenion, a general of Cleopatra in command of her forces there, and an enemy of Herod. He had his plan prepared as he watched to see the outcome, having decided that if the Arabs pulled off a brilliant victory he would take no action, but if they were defeated, as in fact happened, he would attack the Jews with a force of local people who had joined his ranks.

117   So at that moment he fell upon Herod's men without warning, when they were exhausted and believed themselves the victors, and carried out a great slaughter. The Jews, who had spent all their fighting spirit on their

declared enemy and were enjoying their victory with no
fear of danger, were quickly overcome by their attackers,
and they suffered heavy losses on the rocky terrain, which
was unsuitable for horses and more familiar to their new
118 enemy. And with the Jews in these difficulties, the Arabs
took heart and rallied and began to kill them when they
were already routed, and those who died met death in
119 many forms. Of those who escaped, only a few found
refuge in their camp. King Herod, despairing of the battle,
rode off to get help, but for all his haste he was too late to
save the Jewish camp from capture. The Arabs, however,
were extremely fortunate to have won such an unexpected
victory, which had been far from their grasp, and to have
wiped out a large part of their enemy's army.

120   From then on Herod had recourse to guerrilla tactics,
overrunning much of the Arabs' territory and causing
damage by his raids. He camped in the hills, always
avoiding an open engagement, but still inflicting considerable losses by his continual and unremitting harassment.
In this way he looked after his own men while doing all
he could to recover from his setback.

121   Meanwhile the Battle of Actium took place between
Caesar and Antony, in the seventh year of Herod's reign,
and the land of the Jews suffered an earthquake of unprecedented violence, which caused great destruction of the
122 country's cattle. About thirty thousand people also per-
ished under the ruins of their houses, although the army,
which was camped in the open, was not harmed in the
disaster.

123   The Arabs were given an exaggerated report of what
had happened by people intent on gratifying their hatred
of the Jews, and the news made them arrogant, in the
belief that their enemy's land was ruined, his people
destroyed, and that no opposition to them now survived.
124 And so they seized and killed the Jewish envoys who had
come to make peace with them in the changed circumstances, and then, full of confidence, marched against their
125 army. The Jews offered no resistance to their attack, and
were so disheartened by their misfortunes that they gave
up their cause as altogether hopeless. They despaired of
fighting on equal terms after their defeats in the earlier

battles, and equally of getting help from outside while
their country lay in ruins.

126   In this emergency, the king addressed his officers in an
attempt to boost their morale and raise their fallen spirits,
and only after inspiring some of the better sort with a new
courage did he venture to speak to the common soldiers.
He had hesitated to address them before for fear of finding
them unresponsive because of their reverses, but he now
made his appeal to the rank and file, in the following
words.

127   I am well aware, men, that our efforts have encountered
many obstacles over this difficult time, and in such circumstances even men of exceptional courage are likely to lose
128   heart. But we have a fight on our hands, and nothing has
happened that cannot be put right by a single successful
action. And so, to put you in good heart, I have decided to
set out the reasons why that proud spirit of yours should
remain unbowed.

129   I want first to speak of the war, and to show that we
have justice on our side, as we have been forced into it by
the outrages committed by the enemy; for if you understand
this, it will be your chief inspiration. And next I propose to
show you that there is nothing to be feared in our position,
and that we have every reason to hope for victory.

130   I shall begin with the first point, and call you as witnesses
of what I have to say. You are, of course, familiar with the
Arabs' disrespect for law, and that treachery in their dealings with all nations which we would expect from a barba-
rous people with no idea of God. But their chief quarrel is
with us; their motives are greed and envy, and their tactics
a sudden ambush in our moment of confusion.

131   But why should I waste words? When they were threatened with losing their independence, and with enslavement
to Cleopatra, who but we freed them from fear? It was my
friendship with Antony and his regard for us that saved
them from an irreparable reverse, as the great man was
wary of taking any measure that might arouse our sus-
132   picion. It is true that he wished to transfer certain parts of
our two dominions to Cleopatra, but again it was I who
managed this, and by the many gifts I gave him from my

private means I obtained security for both peoples. I took personal responsibility for the payments, giving two hundred talents myself and standing surety for two hundred more, which are included in her revenue but withheld from us by these Arabs.

133   Yet it was not right that the Jews should pay tribute, or surrender part of their land, to any man on earth; and even if it were, we certainly have no reason to pay for these people, whom we ourselves have preserved. The Arabs made this agreement, and believed at first that they had won a very favourable concession: so how can it be right for them to cheat us of these payments, especially when we

134   were not enemies, but friends? If there is room for good faith even towards one's worst enemies, then certainly there is an absolute duty to keep faith with one's friends. But for the Arabs no such principle exists; they believe profit, by whatever means obtained, to be the highest good, and see no harm in doing wrong, if only they can profit by it.

135   So is there still any question in your minds whether we should punish the transgressors? It is the will of God, who commands us always to hate lawlessness and injustice; and

136   the war we are engaged in is not only just but an obligation on us. They have perpetrated what Greeks and barbarians alike agree to be the worst possible offence against the law, by cutting the throats of our ambassadors. The Greeks have declared heralds to be sacred and inviolate, while we have learned the noblest of our doctrines and the holiest part of our law from messengers sent by God.* The name of herald can reveal God to mankind and reconcile enemy with

137   enemy. What greater sacrilege could there be, therefore, than to kill ambassadors whose mission was to negotiate a just peace? And after committing such crimes, how could they expect to enjoy a prosperous life, or success in warfare? In my judgement, this is impossible.

138   What if someone objects that, while godliness and justice are on our side, yet they have the advantage in courage or numbers? I reply, first, that you have no right to say this; for those who have justice on their side have God on their side, and where God is, there too are both numbers and courage.

139   But let us also examine our own record. We won the first

battle. In the second engagement, they offered no resistance and fled at once, with no answer to our determined assault. We were already victorious when Athenion fell upon us and 140 started an undeclared war. Is this a sign of their valour, or a second example of their crookedness and treachery? Why should our spirits droop when the facts ought to strengthen our hopes? How can we be cowed by men like these? When they fight an honest contest, they are always beaten, and 141 their so-called victories are achieved by dishonest means. If anyone thinks them brave, surely this very thought should put new heart into him? True valour appears not in attacking those who are weaker, but in the ability to master even a stronger enemy.

142   As for our own sufferings and the effects of the earthquake, if any of you feel demoralised by these, there are two points you should bear in mind. First, the Arabs have an exaggerated account of the facts, and this has led them to miscalculate. Second, it would be dishonourable if the same events that inspire boldness in them were to make 143 cowards of us. They get their courage not from any native virtue of their own, but from their hope that we are already broken by our misfortunes, and if we march against them, we shall shatter their confidence and regain the advantage of fighting a disheartened enemy.

144   We have not in fact been so badly hurt, nor is the wrath of God responsible for what has happened, as some suppose. No, these are mere accidents and chance misfortunes. And if they occurred in accordance with God's will, clearly they have ceased in accordance with His will, and He is satisfied with what is past. If He had wished to harm us further, He would not have changed.

145   That He wishes this war to be pursued and knows it to be just, He has Himself revealed. In the earthquake, while people were dying throughout the country, not a man on armed service came to harm. Every one of you was spared, and by this God makes it plain that, even if you took your children and your wives into battle with you, you would suffer no great hurt.

146   Bear this in mind, and – what is more important – remember that at every moment you have God as your protector. Go out to the attack, and let the justice of your

cause give you courage. There awaits you an enemy who betrays friendship, violates truces, commits sacrilege against ambassadors, and who can never be your match in valour.

147   After listening to this speech the Jews looked forward to the battle with buoyed spirits, and when he had made the customary sacrifices Herod led them at speed against the Arabs and crossed the River Jordan.

148   Encamping near the enemy, he determined to capture a stronghold that lay between the two lines, and which he reckoned would serve to his advantage, either as a base from which to launch a surprise attack, or as a fortified

149 camp if battle had to be deferred. The Arabs had the same intention, and a fight began for possession of the post. At first there was no more than a skirmish, but as they came to close quarters the casualties mounted on both sides until the Arabs were defeated and withdrew.

150   At this, Jewish hopes at once soared, and reckoning that the enemy would do anything rather than join battle, Herod began the more boldly to tear down their palisades and move in to attack their camp. His tactics proved sound, for when the Arabs were forced out they advanced

151 in disorder, utterly demoralised and despairing of victory. Even so, they engaged hand to hand, since they had the advantage of numbers and found a new boldness under the dictate of necessity; and in the stubborn battle that ensued many fell on either side, until the Arabs at last were put to flight.

152   Once they gave way a great slaughter took place, since they not only fell at the enemy's hands, but compounded their losses in the disorderly rout by trampling one another

153 and falling on their own weapons. As a result, five thousand of them were left dead. The rest succeeded in reaching the shelter of their entrenchment, but had no sure hope of survival through lack of provisions, and especially of

154 water. The Jews pursued them but failed to storm the camp. Instead, they surrounded the palisade and kept watch, preventing help from entering and making it impossible to escape.

155   Finding themselves in such straits, the Arabs sent ambassadors to Herod, first to discuss a truce, and then, so

pressing was their thirst, to offer unconditional surrender as the price of obtaining immediate relief from their dis-

156 tress. But he rejected their overtures, refusing a ransom for his prisoners and any other reasonable terms, implacable in his desire to get revenge for their crimes against the Jews. And so they were forced by thirst and their other privations to come out and deliver themselves into captivity.

157 Over the course of five days, four thousand men in all were captured in this way; but on the sixth day all those who were left decided to resume hostilities and make a sally against their enemy, preferring even to die in the attempt than to perish ingloriously one by one. With this

158 resolve they came out from their entrenchment but, demoralised and physically weak as they were, they proved quite unequal to the contest. Having no hope of distinguishing themselves they reckoned it an advantage to die and a misfortune to live, and some seven thousand of them fell in the battle.

159 After this crushing defeat their former spirit deserted them, but they admired the leadership that Herod showed in the face of his own reverses, and for the future submit-

160 ted to him and proclaimed him protector of their nation. And Herod, full of pride at his successes, returned to his own country, his reputation greatly enhanced by this latest proof of his valour.

The Execution of Hyrcanus

161 In general Herod's affairs were now prospering, and his position altogether unassailable. But Antony's defeat by Caesar in the Battle of Actium presented a new danger and put at stake the whole future of his reign. At that

162 moment his situation seemed desperate, both to Herod himself and his associates, whether enemies or friends, as it seemed unlikely that he would go unpunished for his

163 close friendship with Antony. His friends, therefore, abandoned all hope for him, while his enemies made a show of sympathising, but secretly felt pleased at the prospect of better times to come.

164 As for Herod, seeing that no one of royal rank remained

except Hyrcanus, he thought that it would now serve his interests to put him out of the way. If he survived and escaped the danger he was in, he would thereby insure himself against a bid for the kingship, at such a difficult time for himself, by a man who had a better claim to it; while if he suffered death at Caesar's hand, envy made him want to remove the only man who might succeed to his throne.

165   While he was occupied with these thoughts, an opportunity was afforded him by his opponents. Hyrcanus himself was a man of peaceable disposition who chose not to meddle in affairs of state or engage in subversive activities, and was content to acquiesce in whatever for-
166   tune brought about. Alexandra, however, who was contentious and obsessed with her hope of a change of government, kept urging her father not to tolerate indefinitely Herod's criminal treatment of their family, but to take the initiative in securing their future hopes. And she
167   begged him to write of this to Malchus, the ruler of the Arabs, and ask him to receive them and conduct them to safety, arguing that if they got away and Herod were to suffer the likely fate of an enemy of Caesar's, they would be the only candidates for the royal power, both because of their lineage and because of their popularity with the mass of the people.

168   Despite her efforts to persuade him, Hyrcanus continued to reject her proposals. But Alexandra had the argumentative nature of a woman, and never left off by night or day from speaking to him about this and about Herod's treacherous designs against them; and in the end he gave way and agreed to give a letter to Dositheus, a friend of his, in which he arranged for the Arab to send him horsemen to escort them to Lake Asphaltitis,* three hun-
169   dred stades from the borders of Jerusalem. He trusted Dositheus, since he was a loyal servant to himself and Alexandra and had no small reason to hate Herod, being a relative of Joseph, whom Herod had killed, and a brother of men murdered earlier at Tyre by Antony.

170   Yet these grievances were not enough to ensure Dositheus's loyalty to Hyrcanus, as he entertained hopes of still greater rewards from the king, and he handed over

171 the letter to Herod. The king acknowledged the favour, and requested him to oblige him further by giving the letter, folded and sealed, to Malchus and bringing back his written response, as it was of great importance to him

172 to know the Arab's mind as well. Dositheus willingly performed this service, and the Arab sent back the reply that he would receive Hyrcanus and his companions and all his Jewish sympathisers, and would send soldiers to escort them safely, promising that Hyrcanus would lack nothing that he asked for.

173 When Herod received this letter, he at once sent for Hyrcanus and questioned him about the terms of the agreement he had made with Malchus; and when the other denied it, he showed the letters to the Sanhedrin and had the man put to death.

174 Our account of these events is the one contained in King Herod's memoirs, but the other sources give a different version. They deny that Herod had such grounds as these for killing Hyrcanus, and say that he accused him after laying a trap for him with characteristic treachery.

175 They tell how Herod at a banquet asked Hyrcanus, without arousing his suspicion, whether he had had any letters from Malchus; and when Hyrcanus admitted to

176 having received written messages of greeting from him, he asked him further if he had taken any gift of his. Hyrcanus replied that Malchus had sent him nothing more than four horses for riding, but Herod construed this as evidence of venality and treason, and ordered the man to be strangled.

177 But as proof that Hyrcanus was guiltless of any crime when he met this end, the sources refer to his inoffensive character, and the fact that even in his youth he gave no sign of a headstrong or impulsive disposition, nor again when he was king; for while he reigned he delegated most

178 of the administration to Antipater. He was, moreover, at that time eighty-one years old,* and knew that Herod's power was impregnable; and he had crossed the Euphrates, leaving the people beyond that river who held him in honour, in order to submit entirely to Herod's authority. That he should have had any hand in revolution, therefore, they regard as quite incredible and out of keeping with his

character and they dismiss these charges as a pretext
invented by Herod.

179   This was the death that befell Hyrcanus, after a life of
mixed and varied fortunes. At the very beginning of his
mother Alexandra's reign* he was appointed high priest
180 of the Jewish nation and held the office for nine years. On
his mother's death* he succeeded to the throne, but after
a reign of three months was deposed by his brother
Aristobulus. Restored to power by Pompey, he recovered
all his honours and enjoyed them for forty years, before
181 being ousted a second time by Antigonus,* suffering muti-
lation and becoming a prisoner of the Parthians. In time
he returned from there to his own country because of the
hopes held out to him by Herod, but all his expectations
were disappointed.

His life was dogged by misfortunes, and the bitterest of
them, as we have said, was that in old age he met an
182 unworthy end. For he seems to have been in all respects a
decent and fair-minded man, and to have ruled by delegat-
ing most of the business of government to his officials,
having no great interest in public affairs and lacking the
ability to govern a kingdom. Antipater and Herod owed
their advancement to his good nature, and the end he met
at their hands was an offence against both justice and
piety.

Friend of Caesar

183 After disposing of Hyrcanus, Herod was anxious to visit
Caesar. Because of his past friendship with Antony he
could not hope that his cause would find favour, and he
was suspicious of Alexandra, fearing that she would seize
the opportunity to stir up revolt among the people and
184 plunge the kingdom into civil war. And so he put his
brother Pheroras in complete charge of affairs, with
instructions to carry on the government if they had bad
185 news of him, and moved his mother Cypros, his sister and
all his children to Masada. As for his wife Mariamme, her
quarrel with his mother and sister made it impossible for
her to stay with them, and so he moved her to Alexandreion with her mother Alexandra, leaving in charge there

his steward Joseph and Soemus the Ituraean. These men, who had been utterly loyal to him from the first, he left behind on that occasion to keep the women under surveil-
186 lance, while representing it as a mark of honour; and they were ordered, if the news of him was bad, to kill both women immediately and do all in their power to keep the kingdom for his sons and his brother Pheroras.

187 After giving these instructions Herod made haste to Rhodes to meet Caesar. When his ship put in at the city he removed his diadem, but otherwise retained all the dignity of his rank, and on meeting Caesar and obtaining leave to speak with him he displayed his proud spirit still
188 more. He disdained the role of suppliant, which in the circumstances he might have been expected to take, and declined to plead for mercy, as if in admission of his guilt. Instead, he gave his account of his actions without fear of the consequences.

189 He told Caesar that he had had the greatest friendship for Antony and had done everything he could to help him attain the supreme power. He had not, indeed, taken part in his campaign, owing to the diversion created by the Arabs, but he had sent him money and grain. Yet he said
190 that even these contributions fell short of his real obliga- tion, for when a man acknowledges his friendship for another, whom he knows to be his benefactor, then he has a duty to share his danger with all his heart and strength and all his substance.

In this respect his own conduct had left something to be desired, but he felt sure that he had at least been right not
191 to desert Antony after his defeat at Actium, nor to transfer his hopes to another upon the evident change in Antony's fortune. Moreover, he had proved himself, if not a worthy fellow combatant, at least a most shrewd counsellor to Antony, in advising him that the only way to save himself and retain his power was to destroy Cleopatra.

192 'For once she had been disposed of,' he said, 'he might have kept his power and found it easier to reach agreement with you in place of enmity. But he took no regard of my advice, and chose instead a reckless course of action, to his own undoing and your advantage.

193 'And so, if you now judge my commitment by the anger

you feel towards Antony, I cannot deny what I have done,
nor shall I be ashamed to declare my loyalty to him. But if
you would disregard the individual concerned, and examine how I requite my benefactors and how staunch a friend
I prove, then you may know me by the test of my past
actions. Change but the name, and the very firmness of
my friendship will be enough to win your approval.'

194   With such words as these and by his general demeanour
he displayed a freedom of spirit that Caesar, himself an
honourable and magnanimous man, found particularly
appealing, and so succeeded in turning the grounds on
which he was charged into the foundation of Caesar's
195   goodwill towards him. Caesar restored his diadem to him,
urging him to show himself no less a friend to him than
he had formerly been to Antony, and held him in the
highest honour. He further remarked that a dispatch from
Quintus Didius* had told how Herod had made every
effort to assist him in the matter of the gladiators.

196   After being accorded this favourable reception and realising that, beyond all his hopes, his throne was now more
secure than ever, by the gift of Caesar and a decree of the
Romans which Caesar had obtained in confirmation,
Herod escorted Caesar on his way to Egypt, lavishing gifts
on him and his friends beyond his means and displaying
the utmost generosity. He also made a request that
197   Alexas,* an associate of Antony's, should be spared the
death penalty, but in this he was unsuccessful as Caesar
was already bound by an oath.

198   Herod now returned to Judaea, his honour and assurance greater than before, to confound those who had
anticipated the opposite outcome. It seemed as if by the
grace of God he invariably emerged from danger with his
fame enhanced. He at once prepared for the reception of
199   Caesar, who was about to invade Egypt from Syria; and
when he arrived, Herod received him at Ptolemais with all
the courtesy befitting a king, and supplied his army with
gifts of friendship and abundant provisions.

He was counted among Caesar's most loyal allies, riding
by his side when he reviewed his troops, and providing
quarters for him and his friends in a hundred and fifty
apartments, all furnished for their comfort at lavish

200 expense. And as they crossed the desert he arranged for their needs to be supplied in plenty, so that they had no lack of wine or – even more necessary for the soldiers – of water.

To Caesar personally he gave eight hundred talents, a gift which caused everyone to reflect that his display of loyalty was on a far greater and more splendid scale than
201 his kingdom could afford, but which served to confirm the sincerity of his allegiance. His generosity had been well timed to meet the needs of the moment, and for this he gained particular credit; and when they returned from Egypt, he put himself at their service no less willingly than before.

The Execution of Mariamme

202 However, on his return to his kingdom he found his household in disorder and his wife Mariamme and her
203 mother Alexandra full of resentment. With understandable suspicion they believed that they had been moved to that fortress not for the security of their persons, but to be kept under guard, with no power over others or over their own affairs, and this made them bitter.

204 Mariamme also regarded the king's love as an empty pretence and a deceit which he practised for his own advantage, and recalling his instructions to Joseph, she was indignant at the thought that, even if he came to grief, he had given her no hope of surviving him. Accordingly, she had already begun to court the favour of the guards, and especially of Soemus, whom she knew to be in overall charge.

205 Soemus at first remained faithful to his master and neglected none of Herod's instructions, but his resistance gradually weakened as the women became more persistent
206 and lavished presents on him, and he finally disclosed to them all the king's instructions. He did not in fact expect Herod to return with his former authority intact, and therefore supposed that his behaviour would bring him to no harm at the king's hands, while ingratiating him with the women; and it was reasonable to assume that they would not forfeit their privileged position, but would be

further rewarded either by reigning themselves or by being
207   close to the sovereign. But he was equally optimistic at the
thought that, even if Herod returned with all his purposes
accomplished, he would be unable to refuse his wife
anything that she desired; for Soemus knew the king's love
for Mariamme to be beyond all reason. These were the
motives that induced him to reveal Herod's instructions.

208   His words angered Mariamme, who could see no end to
the dangers with which her husband threatened her, and
in her bitterness she prayed that he would get no justice
from Caesar, reckoning that her life with him would be
unbearable if he were successful. In the event, she made
these feelings plain and concealed none of the emotion
that possessed her.

209   On his return from the voyage that had brought him
such great and unexpected success, it was naturally to his
wife first of all that Herod told the good news, and she
alone of the company whom he honoured with his
embrace, because of his love for her and the intimacy that
had existed between them.

210   But his tale of good fortune brought her no joy, but
resentment rather, a feeling that she found impossible to
conceal. In disdain for him and with the assurance of her
superior birth, she returned his embraces with a groan,
making it clear that she was vexed rather than pleased by
his recital. Her dislike of him, which he had previously
only suspected, was now manifest, and his confusion
deepened.

211   He was dismayed to see his wife's unaccountable and
undisguised hatred for him, and distressed by her attitude,
but his love for her was beyond bearing, and he could not
continue in one mind for long, but swung all the time
between anger and reconcilement, in either mood deeply
212   insecure. Thus entangled between hatred and tenderness,
he was often disposed to repay her disdain, but his heart
was captive and he was too weak to be rid of the woman.
In short, he would gladly have punished her, but was
afraid that if he did so and put her to death he would
unwittingly bring a heavier punishment on himself.

213   When his sister and mother saw his feelings towards
Mariamme, they believed the time was ripe to satisfy their

hatred of her, and they began to gossip and provoke Herod by making serious slanders against her, calculated to excite both his hatred and his jealousy. Herod, while
214 not unwilling to hear such stories, lacked the courage of his conviction to act against his wife; but his attitude towards her hardened, and the resentment was mutual, with Mariamme making no attempt to disguise her feelings, and Herod always vacillating between desire and anger.

215   The consequence would quickly have proved fatal, had not the news just then been brought that Caesar had won the war, and with the death of Antony and Cleopatra was in control of Egypt.* At this, Herod made haste to meet Caesar, leaving his family affairs as they were. As he was
216 about to leave, Mariamme presented Soemus to him, professing to be very grateful for the care he had shown her, and asked the king to make him governor of a local
217 district, and Soemus was granted this honour.

On arriving in Egypt, Herod entered into discussions with Caesar with a new freedom, as he was now his friend, and his rewards were impressive. Caesar gave him four hundred Gauls who had served Cleopatra as bodyguards, and restored to him the territory which she had appropriated, and he annexed to his kingdom Gadara, Hippus and Samaria, and also the coastal cities of Gaza, Anthedon, Joppa and Strato's Tower.

218   His fame enhanced by these acquisitions, Herod escorted Caesar towards Antioch before returning home. But the growing success which he felt in his external affairs was matched by the deterioration of his domestic life, particularly with respect to his marriage, on which above all his happiness had seemed to rest; for he felt for Mariamme a love no less deep than those that are rightly celebrated in story.

219   Mariamme, though otherwise a chaste and faithful wife to him, had a streak of womanly cruelty in her nature and had no inhibitions about mocking his enslavement to passion. With no sense of occasion, she would fail to reflect that she was subject to a king and he her master, and frequently treated him with arrogance, which he affected to disregard and bore with an exaggerated for-

220 bearance. As for his mother and sister, she openly scoffed at their low birth and spoke abusively to them, so that the women's relationship was already one of hostility and
221 irreconcilable hatred. But at this time even more serious slanders were made, feeding suspicion which grew for a whole year from the time of Herod's return from Caesar. In the end, however, the violence suppressed for so long was unleashed. The occasion was as follows.

222 One day at noon the king lay down to rest and called for Mariamme, out of the great tenderness that he always felt for her. She came in, but did not lie down in spite of his urging. Instead, she treated him with disdain and reproached him for killing her father* and brother.
223 Angered by her arrogant manner, Herod was on the point of a violent and precipitate response, and his sister Salome, seeing him to be unusually agitated, sent in his cup-bearer, according to a prearranged plan, with instructions to say that Mariamme had tried to persuade him to help her
224 prepare a love-potion for the king. And if the king should be disturbed and ask what it was, she told him to feign ignorance, and say that the potion was hers and that his task was merely to serve it; while if Herod were unconcerned, he should leave the matter there, and no harm would come to him. She had given him this briefing some time before, and on the present opportunity sent him in to speak his part.
225 He entered with a plausible show of urgency, and said that Mariamme had given him gifts and tried to persuade him to give the king a love-potion. Herod, his suspicion aroused, asked what the love-potion was, and he replied that it was a drug given him by Mariamme, but as he did not know its properties he had decided that the safer course for himself and the king would be to inform him of it.
226 The effect of his words was to provoke Herod to an even worse humour than before, and he proceeded to torture the eunuch, who was utterly loyal to Mariamme, and question him about the drug, knowing that nothing of any significance could have been done without his
227 involvement. But even in his extremity the man had nothing to tell about the matter for which he was being

tortured, although he did say that his wife's hostility to Herod had arisen from information given to her by Soemus.

228   As he said this, the king cried out that Soemus, who had served him most faithfully throughout his reign, would not have betrayed his instructions unless his intimacy with Mariamme had gone further than it should. He gave
229   orders that Soemus should be arrested and put to death at once, while to his wife he conceded the right to a trial.

Summoning his closest advisers he brought a detailed accusation against her concerning the love-potions and drugs which slander alleged that she had prepared. He was beside himself as he spoke, his judgement blinded by rage, and when they perceived his mood the court concluded by
230   condemning her to death. After sentence was passed, the thought occurred to him and to some of the others present that she should not be done away with so hastily, but be imprisoned in one of the strongholds in the kingdom.
231   Salome and her friends, however, made every effort to get rid of the unfortunate woman, and they won the argument with the king by warning him to avoid the popular riots which they predicted if she were allowed to live. And so it came about that Mariamme was led to her death.
232   Alexandra weighed up the situation and felt that she had little hope of escaping a similar fate at Herod's hands. And so she changed her sympathies, reversing the bold stand that she had taken before, and in a particularly
233   unseemly manner. Wishing to make plain her own ignorance of the crimes with which Mariamme was charged, she leaped from her place and reproached her daughter in the hearing of them all, screaming that she had been wicked and ungrateful to her husband and deserved to be punished for her impudence, and that she had failed in her duty to the common benefactor of them all.
234   This hypocritical and indecent performance, during which she made so bold as to seize Mariamme by the hair, naturally incurred the severe condemnation of the others, who saw it as a tasteless piece of play-acting. But none showed their disapproval more plainly than the con-
235   demned woman herself. Mariamme watched her mother's disgusting behaviour without a word or any hint of embar-

rassment, yet showed by her proud bearing how deeply she resented her offensive and grotesque display. And as
236 for herself, she bore herself calmly and kept her complexion as she went to her death, leaving the onlookers in no doubt of her noble breeding even in her last moments.

237 Such was the death of Mariamme, a woman distinguished for her continence and magnanimity of character, though inclined to be unreasonable and excessively quarrelsome. Words cannot do justice to her physical beauty and social presence, in which she surpassed all her contem-
238 poraries; yet this was the principal reason for her failure to please the king and live happily with him. Courted by him constantly because of his love, and anticipating no unkindness at his hands, she had an unbridled tongue. She
239 was distressed by his treatment of her relatives, and saw fit to tell him all her feelings on the matter; and in the end she succeeded in making enemies not only of the king's mother and sister but of Herod himself, the one person whom she completely trusted to do her no harm.

240 But once she was destroyed, the king's desire for her, which we have earlier described, burned still more strongly. For the love he felt for her was never of a tranquil kind, or such as arises from ordinary companionship. It had begun as a divine possession, and the frank intercourse of married life did nothing to check the growth of
241 his passion. But this latest and keenest affliction seemed a kind of divine vengeance for the death of Mariamme, whose name he repeatedly invoked in undignified fits of grief.

To take his mind from her, he thought of every possible diversion and arranged parties and banquets for himself;
242 but it was all to no effect. And so he began to neglect the administration of his kingdom, and became so obsessed by his morbid feelings that he would order his servants to summon Mariamme, as if she were still alive and able to respond.

243 While he was in this state, a plague broke out and destroyed the greater part of the population, including his most honoured friends, a visitation universally attributed to the wrath of God, in retribution for the unlawful killing
244 of Mariamme. This only served to aggravate the king's

condition, and he finally took himself off into the wilderness, where he indulged his grief under the pretence of hunting.

245   But he had not passed many days there when he succumbed to an extremely severe illness. The symptoms included inflammation and pain in the back of his head, and impairment of his reason, and none of the remedies that were tried brought him relief, but rather the reverse.

246   Eventually his condition became desperate, and the doctors attending him, seeing that the disease would not respond to their own medicines and that the king could only follow a course of treatment determined by his illness, decided to give him whatever he felt constrained to ask for, and left the slender hope of his recovery to fortune and the effectiveness of his diet. It was in Samaria, later called Sebaste, that Herod suffered this illness.

The Hasmonaean Opposition Eliminated

247   Alexandra was staying in Jerusalem when she learned of Herod's condition, and took steps to seize control of the

248   two strongholds in the city, one of which protected the city itself, and the other the Temple. Whoever controlled these had the whole nation in his power, since without the command of them it was impossible to offer sacrifice, and to fail in this duty would be quite unacceptable to the Jews, who would rather lose their lives than neglect their customary worship of God.

249   Alexandra therefore proposed to the captains of these guard posts that they should surrender them to her and Herod's sons, to prevent anyone else from seizing power in the event of Herod's death; and if he survived, she promised that no one would keep them more secure for him than his nearest of kin.

250   But they had no patience with her proposals. They had always been loyal to Herod, and never more so than now, as they disliked Alexandra and considered it an impiety to give Herod up for lost while he was still alive. They were in fact old friends of the king, and one of them, Achiab,

251   was also his cousin. And so they immediately sent a

messenger to tell Herod of Alexandra's purpose, and with no delay he gave the order for her to be put to death.

Herod had made a difficult and painful recovery from his illness, which put him in a cruel temper. His mental and physical distress had made him morose and ready to
252 use any pretext to punish those who fell foul of him, and he even killed his closest friends, Costobarus, Lysimachus, Antipater surnamed Gadia, and Dositheus, for the following reason.

253 Costobarus was an Idumaean of high rank, whose ancestors had been priests of Kozai, whom they worship
254 as a god. Hyrcanus had changed their way of life and imposed on them the customs and laws of the Jews.* When Herod became king he appointed Costobarus governor of Idumaea and Gaza, and gave him his sister Salome in marriage, after putting to death her former husband Joseph, as we have related.

255 Costobarus was delighted with these unexpected favours, and his excitement at his good fortune led him to take an increasingly independent line. He thought it wrong that he should be subject to Herod and carry out his orders, and that the Idumaeans should obey the Jews and
256 conform to their customs. Accordingly, he sent to Cleopatra and told her that Idumaea had always belonged to her ancestors, and that she would be justified in asking Antony for their land; and he assured her of his readiness
257 to switch his allegiance to her. He did this, not out of any desire to be ruled by Cleopatra, but because he thought that, with Herod deprived of most of his power, it would be a simple matter for him to establish himself as ruler of the Idumaean nation, and to extend his influence. His ambition knew no bounds, founded as it was on his noble lineage and on the great wealth he had acquired by a lifetime of profiteering, and there was nothing modest about the aims he entertained.

258 Cleopatra therefore asked Antony for this land, but was refused. The negotiations were reported to Herod, who was ready to kill Costobarus, but let him go at the request of his sister and mother, and granted him a pardon. But he remained suspicious of Costobarus from that time because of this initiative.

259   Some time later, Salome had occasion to quarrel with Costobarus, and promptly sent him a bill of divorcement to dissolve their marriage. This was not in accordance with Jewish law, for we permit only the husband to do this, and even a divorced woman has no authority to marry again without the consent of her former husband.

260   But Salome preferred her own authority to the law of her people, renouncing her marriage and telling her brother Herod that it was out of loyalty to him that she had left her husband, as she had learned that Costobarus, together with Antipater, Lysimachus and Dositheus, was planning to revolt. And in support of her charge she stated that for the past twelve years Costobarus had been giving refuge to the sons of Baba.

261   This was indeed true, and the king was astonished to hear it; and he was all the more startled because what she had told him had been completely unexpected. He had once been keen to punish the sons of Baba, who were bitter opponents of his, but now with the long lapse of time they had slipped from his memory.

262   The reason for his enmity and hatred towards them was as follows. When Antigonus was king and Herod was besieging the city of Jerusalem with his army, the privations and miseries suffered by the people under siege were so pressing that many of them were already hailing Herod

263   as their saviour and transferring their hopes to him. But the sons of Baba, men of high rank who had great influence with the masses, continued loyal to Antigonus, and persistently tried to discredit Herod and urged them to defend the ancestral power of their royal family. Such was the policy that they pursued, supposing it to be in their own interests as well.

264   But when the city was captured and Herod took control, Costobarus was assigned the task of blocking the exits and keeping guard over the city, to prevent the escape of citizens who were in debt or opposed to Herod's cause. He knew, however, that the sons of Baba enjoyed the respect and esteem of all the people, and believed that by saving their lives he would ensure an important role for himself in any change of government; and so he rescued them and hid them on his own estate.

265   A suspicion of the truth had occurred to Herod at the
time, but Costobarus swore a solemn oath that he knew
nothing of their whereabouts, and so put the idea from his
mind. Later, when the king issued proclamations offering
a reward and explored every means of tracing them, he
again failed to own up, convinced that if the men were
caught his initial denial would make his punishment inevitable. It was not only out of loyalty, therefore, but by
necessity that he was anxious to keep them hidden.

266   But the king now had the facts from his sister, and sent
soldiers to their reported refuge and had them killed,
together with the group acccused with them. As a consequence, nothing now remained of the family of Hyrcanus,* and Herod's control of his kingdom was absolute,
with no one of rank to oppose his unlawful acts.

Pagan Celebrations

267 As a result Herod began to depart still further from
national custom, and slowly corrupted our traditional way
of life, which till then had been inviolable, by the introduction of foreign practices. Even in later times we suffered
great harm as a result of these policies, with the neglect of
the observances which formerly inspired piety in the
masses.

268   In the first place, he instituted a celebration of athletic
games every four years in honour of Caesar, and built a
theatre in Jerusalem and also a huge amphitheatre in the
plain, both of them conspicuously lavish works but alien
to Jewish custom, which has no use for such buildings and
no tradition of public displays of this kind.

269   Even so, Herod celebrated the festival in the most
splendid fashion, advertising it to the neighbouring
countries and inviting contestants from the entire nation.
Athletes and other classes of competitor were summoned
from every land, attracted by the prizes offered and the
270 glory that victory would bring them. The foremost per-
formers in each event were brought together, since Herod
offered magnificent prizes not only for the gymnastic
events but also to musicians and the players called *thymelikoi*,* and spared no pains to persuade all the most

271 famous of them to attend. He also offered large prizes to
charioteers for races between fours and pairs, and to
mounted riders.

For costliness and magnificence he fully matched the
efforts of other nations in his ambition to create a glorious
272 spectacle. All round the theatre there were inscriptions in
honour of Caesar, and trophies of the nations that he had
conquered in war, all of them made for Herod of pure
273 gold and silver; and as for the equipment, there was no
fine garment or jewelled vessel too precious to be on show
during the presentation of the events. Wild beasts, too,
were provided, as he had collected a large number of lions
274 and other animals of exceptional strength or rarity, and
these were pitted in combat with each other or set to fight
with condemned criminals.

Foreigners were amazed at the expense involved, and
275 entranced by the danger of the spectacle, but to the native
Jews it was a flagrant violation of their hallowed customs.
To them it seemed a manifest impiety to throw people to
the beasts for the entertainment of spectators, and an
impiety to change their customary ways for foreign prac-
276 tices. Nothing, however, offended them so much as the
trophies. They imagined that there were lifelike images
enclosed within the armour, and deeply resented it, as it
was contrary to their national tradition to venerate such
objects.

277 Even Herod could see their agitation, and as he thought
it would be inopportune to force their compliance he tried
persuasion in an attempt to win people over and dispel
their religious scruples, but it was to no avail. Disgusted
by innovations which they found offensive they were loud
and unanimous in their protests, insisting that whatever
else they might tolerate, they could not allow human
images in the city, as it was against their national tradition;
and this was a reference to the trophies.

278 Seeing their indignation, Herod realised that they would
not easily relent without some reassurance, and invited the
most eminent of them to accompany him to the theatre,
where he showed them the trophies and asked what they
279 believed them to be. 'Human images,' they cried – and at
this he ordered the outer decoration to be removed and

revealed the bare wood to them. Once they were stripped, the objects provoked only laughter, and the men were highly amused to think that they had previously taken the ornamentation to be a concealment for representations of the human figure.

280   After Herod had rebutted the popular outcry in this way and defused their feeling of anger, most of them were
281 disposed to forget their resentment, but there were some who persisted in their hostility to these alien practices, believing that the destruction of their nation's customs would be the beginning of great evils. They considered it their sacred duty to take any risk rather than seem to connive at the change in their way of life imposed by Herod's introduction of foreign customs, which revealed him as their king in name alone and in reality the enemy of their whole nation.

282   Among the discontented were ten men from the city who took an oath to risk their lives, hid daggers under
283 their cloaks and planned to assassinate the king. One of them, who had joined the conspiracy out of indignation at the news he had heard, was blind and incapable of taking an active part in the venture, but he made himself ready to share their fate if they came to grief, and the others were greatly inspired by his example.

284   So resolved, they made their way, as agreed, to the theatre. They hoped by a surprise attack to catch Herod himself, but even if they missed him they were confident of killing many of his escort, and reckoned that they would have done enough, though they should die for it, to alert the people and the king himself to the scandal of his policies. This was their purpose, and they were ready to act.

285   But Herod had appointed spies to uncover and report such conspiracies, and one of these found out the whole plot and disclosed it to the king just as he was entering the
286 theatre. Remembering the hatred which most of the people felt for him, and the regular disturbances that his acts provoked, Herod took the reports seriously and retired to his palace, where he summoned the accused men by name.
287 There they were apprehended by his men and caught in the act. They knew they could not escape, but lent dignity

to their inevitable deaths by maintaining their proud spirit to the end.

288   Unashamed of their action and making no attempt to deny it, they showed how they held their daggers at the ready, and justified their conspiracy in the name of honour and piety. Their motive, they said, was not gain nor a personal grudge but concern for their people's way of life, 289 which all men have a duty to defend or die for. Such were the words they used in frank admission of their plot, while the king's men had them surrounded. Then they were led away and, after suffering every torment, put to death.

Not long afterwards, the informer himself was kidnapped by some people who showed their hatred of him by killing him and then tearing him limb from limb and 290 throwing him to the dogs. There were many witnesses to this, but no one reported it until Herod conducted a particularly cruel and ruthless investigation, and some women admitted under torture what they had seen. Those responsible were punished for their temerity, and Herod 291 made their families share their fate; but the resolution of the people and their unshakable faith in their laws made him uneasy. In the interests of security, therefore, he decided to confine the people on every side to prevent their opposition to his rule breaking out in open rebellion.

292   The city was secured for him by the palace in which he lived, and the Temple by the strong fortress called Antonia, which had been built by him.* He now conceived the idea of making Samaria, which he called Sebaste,* into a third bulwark against the whole nation, as he believed 293 the place offered no less security against the country, being only a day's journey from Jerusalem, and that it would be equally useful for guarding both the city and the countryside. He also built a fortress to guard the entire nation on 294 the site formerly called Strato's Tower, which he renamed Caesarea.* In the Great Plain* he gave allotments of land to some of his select cavalrymen, and built a fortress for them at a place called Gaba in Galilee, and also rebuilt Esebonitis in Peraea.

295   These were the successive measures that he devised to strengthen his security, by posting garrisons at intervals throughout the entire nation. His purpose was to eliminate

as far as possible the disturbances which the people, in defiance of his authority, repeatedly made upon the smallest provocation, and to ensure that if any trouble were to start, it would not go undetected, as there would always be soldiers stationed nearby who could discover and suppress it. 296 At that time, when he was intent on fortifying Samaria, he arranged to resettle there many of his former allies in war and many from the neighbouring peoples. He was ambitious to create a new city of his own out of what had previously been an undistinguished place, and especially if his ambition could contribute to his security. He also changed the name, calling the city Sebaste, and divided up the adjoining land, which was the best in the country, among the settlers, so that they could enjoy a prosperous life from the time of their arrival.

297 He enclosed the city in a strong wall, exploiting the natural steepness of the ground to strengthen its defences, and the circuit of the wall, which was twenty stades,* exceeded that of the former site and bore comparison with 298 the most famous cities. In the centre of the city he built a precinct, elaborately decorated, a stade and a half in circumference, and within it erected a temple, among the most renowned for its proportions and beauty. Every device of art was used to embellish the different parts of the city, for while seeing the need for security and making it a fortress on a grand scale by the strength of its surrounding walls, he also gave it an elegance that might stand for posterity as a monument to his love of beauty and humanity.

The Famine

299 In this year, which was the thirteenth of Herod's reign,* the country suffered extreme hardships, whether by the 300 wrath of God or because evil falls like this in cycles. First, there were continuous droughts, and as a result the ground was barren and failed to produce its customary crops. And then, because of the change of diet caused by the lack of grain, disease and eventually the plague were prevalent, 301 and their miseries knew no respite. The effects of the plague, which were severe from the start, were aggravated

by the lack of medical care and nourishment, and the deaths of its victims demoralised the survivors, who lacked the resource to cope with their difficulties.

302   With the fruits of that year destroyed and their stores exhausted, there was nothing left to hope for. Their plight, however, grew worse even than they anticipated, and the famine extended beyond that year when the seed of the crops that survived was also lost, and the earth failed to

303   yield a second time. The straits they were in forced them to try a variety of expedients and the position of the king himself was no less desperate, as he was deprived of the revenues which he received from the land and had spent his money on his ambitious programme of urban recon-

304   struction. There appeared to be no means of easing his problems, for people generally blame their rulers when times are bad, and the famine had made him an object of hatred to his subjects.

305   Faced by such difficulties, Herod made plans to meet the crisis. It would not be easy, as the neighbouring peoples had suffered the same privations and had no grain to sell; and he had no money, even if it were possible to

306   buy small quantities at inflated prices. But it was a matter of honour for him to use every means he could to bring relief.

He cut up all the gold and silver ornaments in his palace, sparing nothing, however carefully constructed and precious for its quality of workmanship, converted it into

307   coinage and sent the money to Egypt, where Petronius was Caesar's prefect. Many people in the same need had come to seek help from Petronius, but as he was a personal friend of Herod and wished to rescue his subjects, he gave them preference in the export of grain and did everything he could to assist its purchase and transportation. He was, in fact, the principal, if not the sole source of the aid they obtained.

308   When the supplies arrived, Herod attributed this relief to his own efforts, and not only won the hearts of his previously hostile subjects but exploited the occasion to the full to demonstrate the friendly and protective nature

309   of his rule. To those able to make their own bread he distributed corn in precisely calculated rations, and as

there were many who were too old or otherwise infirm to work the grain themselves, he provided bakers and had
310 the loaves made for them. He also ensured their protection against the winter, for among their problems was a short-age of clothing, due to the destruction and wholesale consumption of their flocks, which had left them with no wool to use or any other suitable covering.

311 After making these provisions, he set about lending aid to the neighbouring cities and gave seed to the people of Syria, a policy which turned to his great advantage, as his generosity was well timed to produce a good harvest and
312 sufficient food for everyone. The scale of his achievement is shown by the fact that on the approach of harvest he sent no fewer than fifty thousand men, fed and maintained by himself, into the countryside, restoring his ravaged kingdom with unfailing energy and enterprise, and bring-
313 ing no small relief to his equally distressed neighbours. There was no one who approached him in need without obtaining help according to his deserts, and peoples and cities, and individuals also made destitute by providing for their communities appealed to his generosity and had their
314 requests granted. It is calculated that external subsidies accounted for ten thousand cors of grain – a cor being equivalent to ten Attic bushels* – while about eighty thousand went to the population of his own kingdom.

315 Herod's concern for their welfare, and the happy timing of his generosity, made a powerful impression on the Jews themselves, and was widely acclaimed by the other nations, and as a result his people forgot the hatred they had felt for his tampering with the laws and royal tra-dition, and believed that he had made handsome amends in coming to their aid when their lives were endangered.
316 He was held in honour also by foreign nations, and it appears that the indescribable hardships that befell him and ravaged his kingdom did much to give him his good name. In times of distress he had proved magnanimous beyond all expectation, and converted the common people to the view that his real character was revealed, not in the behaviour they had previously experienced, but in the solicitude he had shown to supply their needs.

317 About the same time, he sent an auxiliary force to

Caesar consisting of five hundred picked men from his bodyguard, and Aulus Gellius took them on his campaign to the Red Sea, where they served him with distinction.

Herod's Building Projects

3 1 8   Now that Herod's reign was set on a more prosperous course, he built a palace in the Upper City. The rooms, which he built to an exceptional size, were decorated at great expense with gold, stones and pigments; each had enough couches to accommodate a large number of guests, and they had names to match their dimensions, such as
3 1 9   'Caesar's' or 'Agrippa's'. And he fell in love again and made another marriage, having no scruples about living for his own pleasure.

3 2 0   The occasion of his marriage was as follows. There lived in Jerusalem one Simon, a priest of note, the son of Boethus of Alexandria, and he had a daughter considered to be the most beautiful woman of her day, who was the
3 2 1   talk of Jerusalem.* Herod's interest in her was first roused by these reports, but on seeing her he was stunned by the girl's beauty. He was not prepared to entertain the idea of abusing his power to have the enjoyment of her, as he suspected, and with good reason, that it would be held against him as the violent action of a tyrant; and so he
3 2 2   thought it better to marry the girl. Now Simon was too insignificant to form a royal alliance, but too important to be treated with contempt, and Herod pursued his desire by the more reasonable course of raising their status and enhancing their dignity. Specifically, he promptly deprived Jesus, the son of Phiabi, of the high priesthood and appointed Simon to this office, and then married his daughter.

3 2 3   After his wedding he constructed another fortress in the district where he once defeated the Jews, at the time of his
3 2 4   expulsion from power and the ascendancy of Antigonus. This fortress,* which is about sixty stades from Jerusalem, enjoys a naturally strong situation, ideal for its construction. There is a hill in the vicinity, its summit raised artificially and rounded like a woman's breast, with circular towers at intervals, which is approached by a steep

staircase of two hundred steps, made from specially fashioned stones. Within it there are lavish royal apart-
325 ments, designed for both security and elegance, and around the foot of the hill there are residences, noteworthy for their workmanship and in particular for the costly provision of an aqueduct, as the place lacks a natural supply of water. On the surrounding plain a city, second to none in size, has been built, with the hill as its acropolis.

326 Now that all his affairs were prospering as they should and his hopes finding fulfilment, Herod felt not the least misgiving that troubles might arise within the borders of his kingdom. He kept his people in submission by two means, the fear which he inspired by his ruthless use of punishment, and the magnanimity he displayed in taking
327 care of them in emergencies. He also surrounded himself with a cordon of security beyond his borders, as a kind of fortress to protect him against his own subjects, by cleverly cultivating friendly relations with the gentile cities and courting their rulers. To each of them he sent gifts, with a happy timing that increased their gratitude, and employed his natural generosity in the service of his royal power, using every means of strengthening his position while his
328 prosperity continued to grow. But his exertions in this direction, and the flattery that he paid to Caesar and the leading Romans, forced him to depart from the customs of his people and to abuse many of their laws.

329 His ambition led him to found cities and erect temples in them, although he built these in foreign territory beyond his borders, and not in the land of the Jews – we are forbidden to honour statues and sculpted images in the Greek fashion, and the people would not have tolerated it.
330 To the Jews his defence was that he was not acting on his own initiative but in obedience to orders, while he sought to gratify Caesar and the Romans by saying that to honour them was an aim he cherished even above the customs of his own people. His overriding aim, however, was to glorify himself, and his ambition was to leave to posterity ever more imposing monuments of his reign; and this was the spur that drove him to build cities and lavish such enormous expense on the work.

331   His attention was attracted by a place on the coast, an excellent site for a city, formerly called Strato's Tower, and he set about planning it on a magnificent scale. The buildings he erected were of no perfunctory workmanship but everywhere of white marble, and he graced his city with sumptuous palaces and civic halls. He also provided it with a sheltered harbour the size of Piraeus, incorporating landing-places and secondary anchorages. This was

332 the city's most imposing feature, requiring the greatest expenditure of labour, and its construction was particularly remarkable for the fact that the site itself contained no suitable material for such an ambitious project, which was completed at great expense with materials imported from elsewhere.

333   The city is in Phoenicia and lies on the sea route to Egypt, between Joppa and Dora. These are two small coastal towns which offer only poor anchorage because of the prevailing south-west wind, which rolls the sand from the seabed on to the beach and prevents a smooth landing, so that merchants are usually forced to ride at anchor

334 offshore. To overcome this natural disadvantage, Herod laid out a circular harbour, wide enough for large fleets to lie at anchor close to land, by sinking large blocks of stone to a depth of twenty fathoms. Most of these blocks were fifty feet long and no less than eighteen feet wide and nine

335 feet in depth, although there were some larger and some smaller. This mole set in the sea was two hundred feet across. For half its length it served as a barrier against the incoming waves, holding back the flood of the tide, and so was called a breakwater; while the rest of it was topped

336 by a stone wall with towers at intervals, the largest of which, a very fine structure, was named Drusus after Caesar's stepson Drusus, who died young.*

337   Built into the mole were a series of vaulted recesses offering shelter for mariners, and fronting them a wide quay encircled the entire harbour, affording a very pleasant promenade for those so inclined. The entrance or mouth of the harbour faces north, since the north wind

338 brings the clearest weather. At the foundation of the whole circular structure, on the left to those sailing into the harbour, was a broad solid tower designed to offer stout

resistance to the waves, while on the right were two great blocks of stone, larger than the tower opposite, standing upright and clamped together.

339   The land around the harbour was entirely built up with houses of brightly polished stone, and on an elevation in the centre there stood a temple of Caesar, visible from a distance to ships entering the harbour, in which statues of Rome and of Caesar were enshrined. The city itself is called Caesarea, an architectural achievement of great beauty by reason of its stone and the quality of its workmanship.

340   Under the city there were drains and sewers designed no less elaborately than the superstructure. Some of these, laid at equal distances, led into the harbour and the sea, and all were connected by a tunnel running crosswise, so that the rain and the waste from the houses were conveniently discharged together. At high tide the sea flowed through these passages and flushed the whole city.

341   Herod also built within the city a theatre of stone, and on the south side of the harbour, behind the city, an amphitheatre with room for a large crowd of spectators and conveniently situated for a view over the sea. So the city was completed in the space of twelve years, during which the king never wearied of his work or failed to meet the expenses.

Augustus Enlarges Herod's Dominions

342   At this point, with the city of Sebaste also completed, he decided to send his sons Alexander and Aristobulus to
343   Rome to introduce themselves to Caesar. When they arrived in the capital they lodged at the house of Pollio, a particularly warm friend of Herod's, but they were also allowed to stay with Caesar himself, who received the boys with every kindness. He authorised Herod to secure his kingdom on whichever of his children he wished, and also gave him the territory of Trachonitis, Batanaea and Auranitis.*

344   The reason for this was that a certain Zenodorus had leased the estate of Lysanias,* but being dissatisfied with the revenues was supplementing his income by employing

bands of robbers in Trachonitis. The region was inhabited by desperadoes who plundered the property of the Damascenes, and Zenodorus did nothing to stop them but took

345 a share of the profits himself. The neighbouring peoples who were affected by this protested to Varro, who was then governor, and asked him to write to Caesar about Zenodorus's misconduct; and Caesar, on receiving his report, replied that he should drive out the robbers and assign the territory to Herod, so that through his supervision Trachonitis would no longer be a nuisance to its neighbours.

346 It was no easy task to stop them, as they had made brigandage their way of life and had no other means of supporting themselves. They owned neither city nor fields, but only underground dens and caves where they lived together with their cattle. They had managed to collect supplies of water and stores of food and were capable of holding out for a very long time in their secret lair. The

347 entrances were narrow, admitting only one person at a time, but the interiors were incredibly large and constructed to provide plenty of space, and the ground above their homes had no great depth, as the roofs were virtually level with the surface. There were hard rocks everywhere and access was difficult except by following a path with the help of a guide – for not even the paths were straight, but full of twists and turns.

348 It was the habit of these people, when they were restrained from preying on their neighbours, to rob each other instead, so that their way of life encompassed every kind of crime. But Herod, on receiving this grant from Caesar, entered the country with the help of experienced guides, put a stop to their villainy and brought peace and security to the surrounding peoples.

349 Zenodorus was indignant at being deprived of his eparchy,* and even more indignant through envy of Herod taking his place. He went to Rome, therefore, to make charges against him, but returned unsuccessful.

350 About this time Agrippa was sent as Caesar's representative to the countries beyond the Ionian Sea, and while he was wintering in Mytilene Herod, who was one of his

351 closest friends and associates, visited him there, and then

returned to Judaea. Some people from Gadara came to Agrippa with accusations against Herod, but he sent them in chains to the king without even granting them a hearing. And the Arabs also, who had long been resentful of Herod's rule, were in an angry mood and attempted to challenge his authority.

352   This time they believed they had every justification, as Zenodorus, despairing of his own position, had forestalled Herod by selling Auranitis, part of his eparchy, to the Arabs for fifty talents. The district was included in Caesar's gift to Herod, but the Arabs argued that they were deprived of it unfairly and contested Herod's title, mounting frequent raids in the hope of taking it by force as well
353   as having recourse to legal proceedings. They also won over the poorer class of Herod's soldiers, who bore a grudge against him and always entertained hopes of revolution – the favourite resort of those whom life has treated harshly. Herod had been aware of this subversion for some time, but avoided taking reprisals which would give them grounds for causing trouble. Instead, he shrewdly tried to pacify them.

354   On the completion of the seventeenth year of Herod's reign,* Caesar came to Syria. On this occasion most of the inhabitants of Gadara denounced Herod for his oppressive demands and tyrannical rule. They ventured
355   to make these complaints because Zenodorus was most vigorous in bringing charges against him, and swore that he would never give up until, by one means or another, he had had them removed from Herod's kingdom and
356   attached to Caesar's province. Emboldened by these assurances, the Gadarenes were loud in their protests, encouraged by the fact that the men handed over by Agrippa had not been punished, as Herod had released them unharmed. Indeed, it was true of Herod more than any other ruler that while he seemed implacable towards his own people, he was magnanimous in pardoning the misdeeds of foreigners.

357   They accused him, then, of acts of violence and pillage and the destruction of temples; but Herod, quite unruffled, was prompt with his defence, and Caesar grasped his hand
358   in friendship, his good opinion of him in no way altered

by the clamour of the crowd. On the first day speeches
were made relating to these charges, but the hearing went
no further. The Gadarenes, seeing the sympathies of Caesar and his court, expected, with good reason, to be
handed over to the king; and fearing torture they took
their own lives, some by cutting their throats during the
night, some by throwing themselves from heights, and
359 others by falling into the river. This was taken to be an
admission of their presumption and guilt, and as a consequence Caesar acquitted Herod of the charges without
delay.

His good fortune was augmented by another happy
accident. Zenodorus suffered a ruptured intestine, accompanied by severe haemorrhage, and departed this life at
360 Antioch in Syria, and Caesar gave his considerable
domains to Herod. The land lay between Trachonitis and
Galilee, and contained Ulatha and Paneas and the country
round about. He also brought Herod into partnership
with the procurators of Syria, whom he instructed to
obtain Herod's consent in everything they did.

361   Altogether Herod had risen to such a height of prosperity that he enjoyed the special favour of the two rulers of
the mighty Roman empire, Caesar and, second to him,
Agrippa. Next to Agrippa there was no one whom Caesar
honoured more than Herod, while Agrippa gave Herod
362 the first place in his friendship after Caesar. With the
freedom that their esteem made possible he now asked
Caesar for a tetrarchy for his brother Pheroras, and allot-
ted him a revenue of a hundred talents from his kingdom.
This was a safeguard for him, in the event of Herod's
death, and a precaution against the seizure of the land by
Herod's sons.

363   He then escorted Caesar to the sea and, on his return,
built him a most beautiful temple of white marble in the
364 territory of Zenodorus, near the place called Paneion. In
the mountains here there is a lovely cave, and in it an
abrupt and inaccessible chasm filled with still water. The
mountain* towers above it, and below the cave rise the
springs of the River Jordan. It is a celebrated spot, and
Herod gave it a new distinction by dedicating his temple
to Caesar there.

Measures to Encourage Obedience

365 It was also at this time that Herod remitted to his subjects one-third of their taxes, officially to enable them to recover from the famine, but more particularly to regain the loyalty of a disaffected people. They resented innovations likely to result in the destruction of their religion and the disappearance of their way of life. Everywhere there was talk of it, and they were in an angry and restless mood.

366 Herod kept the situation under the closest surveillance, depriving them of any opportunity to make disturbances and commanding them to be busy at their work at all times. In the city people were forbidden to hold meetings and to walk or pass their time in groups, and their every movement was observed. There were harsh punishments for those who were caught, and many were taken, either openly or in secret, to the fortress of Hyrcania, where they were killed. Spies were posted both in the city and on the open roads to keep an eye on people meeting together,

367 and they say that even Herod himself did not neglect to play this role – he would often dress like an ordinary citizen and mingle with the crowds by night, to test their opinion of his rule.

368 Those who remained obdurate and absolutely refused to adapt themselves to the new ways he subjected to every kind of persecution, and from the rest of the population he demanded an oath of allegiance, requiring them to swear to maintain their loyalty to his rule. Most of them

369 complied with his demand from deference or fear, but there were some with enough courage to protest at the enforcement of the oath, and these he got rid of by one

370 means or another. He tried to persuade even Pollio the Pharisee and Samaias and most of their disciples to take the oath, but they would not consent to it; yet they were not punished like the other objectors, but treated respectfully on Pollio's account.

371 Also granted exemption from this injunction were those whom we call Essenes, a sect who follow a way of life revealed to the Greeks by Pythagoras.* I shall tell of the

372 Essenes more fully elsewhere. Hoewever, I ought to explain Herod's reason for honouring the Essenes, whom

he held in higher esteem than their mortal nature required; and my account will be appropriate to a work of history, revealing as it will the reputation of these people.

373   There was a certain Essene named Menachem, whose goodness was attested by the whole tenor of his life, and above all by his foreknowledge of the future, a gift of God. This man once noticed Herod, who was still a boy, going to visit his tutor, and addressed him as 'King of the

374 Jews'. Herod supposed that he did not know who he was, or else was teasing him, and reminded him that he was an ordinary citizen.

But Menachem, with a gentle smile, smacked his bottom and said, 'But you will be king, I tell you, and you will have a prosperous reign, for God has deemed you worthy of it. And remember the smacking that Menachem gave you, and let it be a symbol for you of how life's for-

375 tunes can change. Your best course would be to love justice and piety towards God and to be merciful to your people. But I know that you are not going to be that kind of man, since I understand the whole story. In good

376 fortune you will surpass all other men, and attain to everlasting glory, but you will forget piety and justice. But this cannot escape God's notice, and at the close of your life He will remember it against you, and you will feel His wrath.'

377   At the time Herod took little notice of his words, having no hope of fulfilling them; but after his gradual rise to kingship and prosperity, when at the height of his power, he summoned Menachem and questioned him about the length of time he would reign.

378   Menachem told him nothing; and as he remained silent Herod asked if his reign had no more than ten years to run. 'Twenty or thirty,' he replied, though without fixing a limit to the time. But Herod was satisfied with his answer, and gave him his hand and let him go, and from that moment he always held all the Essenes in honour.

379   This story may seem difficult to believe, but we have thought it right to acquaint our readers with it, and to make known what has occurred among us, because many of this sect, because of their virtue, have been permitted to have a knowledge of divine mysteries.

The Rebuilding of the Temple

380 It was at this time, in the eighteenth year of Herod's reign, and after the events mentioned above, that he undertook the extraordinary task of rebuilding, at his own expense, the Temple of God, extending its precincts and raising it to a height more in keeping with its dignity. He believed that this work, when completed, would be the most glorious of all his achievements, as indeed it was, fit to ensure him an everlasting memorial.

381 Conscious, however, that the people were not prepared for a project of this magnitude and would not readily give their co-operation, he decided to make a speech outlining his entire proposal and enlisting their support for its execution. And so he called them together and spoke as follows.

382 Fellow countrymen, I consider it unnecessary to speak of the past achievements of my reign, except to remark that any prestige they have brought me is less important than
383 their contribution to your security. In the worst hardships I have not failed to meet your needs; my building schemes have been designed not so much for my own safety as for the protection of you all; and I believe that by God's will I have advanced the Jewish nation to a degree of prosperity
384 such as it had never known before. As to the separate structures completed in this country, and the cities we have raised here and in the lands annexed by us, works of great beauty by which we have enhanced the glory of our race – all this you know, and I see no need to elaborate on it.

But the project I now intend to undertake surpasses any
385 of our time in the holiness and beauty of its conception, as I shall now explain. This Temple* here was built by our fathers to the Most High God after their return from Babylon, but in comparison with the first Temple built by Solomon it lacks sixty cubits in height.

386 Now let no one condemn our fathers for neglecting their pious duty – it was not on their account that the Temple stands no higher. The proportions of the building were set by Cyrus and Darius, the sons of Hystaspes, and our fathers were in subjection to them and their descendants, and later

to the Macedonians,* and had no opportunity to restore
the original exemplar of piety to its former height.

387   But today I am your ruler, by the will of God, with the
advantage of a long period of peace, and of a surplus of
wealth and abundant revenues, and above all the friendship
and goodwill of the Romans, the masters of the world. I
propose, therefore, to try to make good the fault which the
subjection of that former time made necessary, and to offer
the completed work of piety to God in full requital for His
gift of this kingdom.

388   These were Herod's words, but his speech caught them
unprepared and sent a shudder through the crowd. Their
doubts concerning the fulfilment of his hopes left them
unperturbed, but they were dismayed that he might demolish the whole edifice without having the means to
bring his project to completion. They thought the risk
too great, and the scale of the enterprise too vast to be
manageable.

389   In response to their misgivings the king tried to reassure
them by declaring that he would not pull down the Temple
until everything needed for its completion was ready to
390   hand. And he was as good as his word. He prepared a
thousand wagons to carry the stones, selected ten thousand highly skilled workmen, bought priestly robes for a
thousand priests, and trained some as stonemasons and
others as carpenters. Only after such thorough and energetic preparation did he set about the building.

391   Removing the old foundations, he laid new ones on
which to build his Temple, which was a hundred cubits*
in length and breadth and a hundred and twenty in height
– though this was reduced in time with the sinking of the
foundations. In the time of Nero we decided to raise it
again.*

392   The Temple was built of blocks of hard, white stone,
each about twenty-five cubits in length, eight in height and
393   twelve in width. The elevation of the whole structure, as
of the Royal Portico, was lowest at the sides and highest
at the centre, and this was clearly visible from a distance
of many stades to people in the country and even more to
anyone living opposite or approaching it.

394   The entrance doors, which with their lintels were the same height as the Temple, he adorned with particoloured curtains, featuring purple dyes and pillars embroidered in
395   the design. Above these and beneath the cornice was spread a golden vine with pendent grape-clusters, delighting the eye by its size and artistry and the precious material from which it was fashioned.

396   He surrounded the Temple with great porticoes, all duly proportioned, lavishing more expense on the work than any of his predecessors and gaining an unrivalled reputation for the embellishment he added to the Temple. Both porticoes were supported by a large wall, and the wall
397   itself was the most impressive piece of work ever heard of by man. The hill was a rocky ascent, sloping gently up to
398   its peak at the eastern part of the city. Our king Solomon, with God-given wisdom, first encompassed its summit with great defensive walls, and fortified it lower down, beginning at the foot where a deep ravine surrounds it, with massive rocks fastened together with lead.

The deeper the wall went the more he removed of the earth inside, and the result was a square structure of
399   immense mass and height, its outward surface revealing the size of the stones, which on the inside were firmly secured by iron clamps to hold the joints permanently in
400   place. Where the work reached the top of the hill, he levelled off the summit and filled in the cavities next to the wall, making the ground flat and equal in height to the upper surface of the wall. Such was the entire circuit of the wall, which measured four stades in circumference, each side having a length of one stade.

401   Inside it and on the very summit there ran another stone wall, with a double portico of the same length as the wall along the eastern ridge. The portico faced the doors of the
402   Temple, which it enclosed, and had been adorned by many earlier kings. All round the Temple precinct were fixed spoils captured from the gentiles, and all these were dedicated by King Herod, who added those that he had taken from the Arabs.

403   At a corner on the north side there stood a citadel, well fortified and of extraordinary strength. It had been built by Herod's predecessors, the kings and high priests of the

Hasmonaean family, who called it their Fortress,* and it
was there that they kept the priestly vestment, which the
404 high priest puts on only when he has to offer sacrifice.
King Herod kept the robe safe there and after his death
the Romans had charge of it until the time of Tiberius
405 Caesar. During his reign Vitellius, the governor of Syria,
came to visit Jerusalem,* where the people gave him a
most splendid reception. He wished to repay their generosity in some way, and when they appealed for permission
to keep the sacred robe under their own authority he
wrote of the matter to Tiberius Caesar. Tiberius gave his
consent, and the Jews retained their authority over the
robe until the death of King Agrippa. After his reign,
406 Cassius Longinus, who was governor of Syria at the time,
and Cuspius Fadus, the procurator of Judaea, ordered the
Jews to deposit the robe in the citadel of Antonia, saying
407 that the Romans ought to have charge of it, as they had
before. The Jews accordingly sent ambassadors to appeal
to Claudius Caesar about the turn of events, and on their
arrival the younger King Agrippa, who happened to be in
Rome, interceded with the emperor and obtained authority
over the robe; and Claudius sent this command to Vitel-
408 lius, who was now legate of Syria.* Previously it had been
under the seal of the high priest and treasurers, and the
day before a festival the treasurers used to go to the
commander of the Roman garrison, examine their own
seal, and take the robe. They would then return it to the
same place when the festival was over, show the commander a seal that tallied with the other, and deposit the
robe again.

409   This digression has been made because of the unfortunate circumstances that occurred later. But at the time of
my narrative, Herod, King of the Jews, strengthened this
citadel for the security and protection of the Temple area,
and as a compliment to Antony, his personal friend and
ruler of the Romans, he called it Antonia.

410   On the western side of the Temple court there stood
four gates. One led to the royal palace by a viaduct over
the intervening valley,* two led to the suburb,* and the
last led to the Upper City, from which it was separated by
long flights of steps going down into the valley and up the

opposite side. The city, shaped like a theatre, lay opposite the Temple, with a deep ravine* running along its entire southern side.

411 The fourth side of the court, facing south, also had gates in it, and above it stood the Royal Portico, with three aisles, stretching from the eastern to the western valley,

412 which set the limits of its length.* No construction under the sun so merits description as this portico. The valley side that supported it was so deep that anyone bending over it from above could not bear to look down to the bottom. But the portico above was also extremely high, and the view from its roof, with the extra height, was enough to cause giddiness, the depths of the valley beneath

413 being out of sight, immeasurably remote. The portico contained four rows of columns, standing at equal distances throughout their length, the fourth row being built into a stone wall. Each column was so wide that it took three men, joining hands with arms outstretched, to encircle it; and the height of the columns, which had a

414 double moulding around the base, was twenty-seven feet. In all they numbered one hundred and sixty-two, and their capitals were sculpted in the Corinthian style, creating a

415 total effect of dazzling magnificence. The four rows divided the space beneath the porticoes into three aisles. Of these, the two outer aisles were constructed in identical proportions, each thirty feet wide, a stade in length and over fifty feet in height, while the middle aisle rose high

416 above them, half as wide again and twice their height. The ceilings were decorated with wood-carvings, deeply cut into a variety of shapes, while the wall at the front of the higher middle aisle had architraves cut into it at either end, resting on pillars which were incorporated in the wall. The entire structure was of polished stone, and an awe-inspiring sight it was – beyond the imagination of those who had not seen it.

417 Such was the first court. A short distance inside it there was a second court,* approached by a few steps and surrounded by a stone balustrade with an inscription

418 forbidding foreigners to enter under pain of death. This inner court on its southern and northern sides had gateways incorporating three separate doors, but towards the

sunrise it had one great gateway, through which those of us who were ritually clean would pass with our wives.

419 Within this second court was the sacred court, prohibited to women, and further within was a third court which only the priests were allowed to enter. In this court stood the Temple, and before it an altar on which we used to sacrifice whole burnt-offerings to God. King Herod did

420 not enter any of these three courts* since he was not a priest and was therefore prohibited, but he occupied himself in the construction of the porticoes and outer courts and completed them in eight years.

421 The Temple itself was built by the priests in a year and six months, and all the people were overjoyed and gave thanks to God, first for the speed of its completion and then for the zeal shown by the king; and they held celebrations and acclaimed the reconstruction. The king

422 sacrificed three hundred oxen to God, and others offered sacrifice according to their means. But to tell the number of these offerings with any accuracy would be an impos-

423 sible task and beyond my powers. As it happened, the Temple was completed on the anniversary of the king's accession, a day on which they regularly held a festival, and the coincidence gave rise to celebrations on a most splendid scale.*

424 An undergound passage was also constructed for the king, leading from Antonia to the inner sacred court at its eastern gate, and above this passage he built himself a tower which he could enter from underground, as a precaution against any popular uprising against the royal

425 house. It is said that throughout the time when the Temple was being built it never rained during the day, but only by night, so that the work was not interrupted; and this story, which our fathers have handed down to us, may well be believed if one considers the other ways in which God manifests His power. Such, then, was the way in which the building of the Temple was completed.

BOOK XVI

Friend of Agrippa

1 In his administration of the government the king was determined to put an end to the various crimes committed in the city and the country, and made a wholly unprecedented law, which he personally enforced, that housebreakers should be sold into slavery and deported from the kingdom. But quite apart from the severity of the sentence for those who suffered it, such punishment

2 involved the violation of ancestral custom; for to be enslaved to foreigners whose way of life was different from that of the Jews, and to be compelled to obey their every command, was an offence against religion and not a penalty for transgressors.

From the earliest times the punishment reserved for such

3 offenders was as follows. The laws required a thief to make fourfold restoration, and if he defaulted he was to be sold into slavery, but certainly not to foreigners nor into lifelong servitude; it was prescribed that he should be

4 released after six years. The new punishment, which was itself a cruel violation of the law, bore the stamp of insolence, an act of retribution conceived by Herod after the manner of a tyrant rather than a king, and in contempt

5 of the interests of his subjects. Its enactment was entirely in character, and contributed to his unpopularity and the complaints made against him.

6 It was at this time that he made a voyage to Italy, from a desire to meet Caesar and to see his sons who were living in Rome, and Caesar gave him a friendly welcome and, as

7 the boys had now completed their studies, allowed him to take them home. When they returned from Italy, the masses took the boys to their heart, and they became the centre of attention both because of the great good fortune

with which they were blessed and because of their truly
royal bearing.

8   This at once aroused the jealousy of Salome, the king's
sister, and of the slanderers who had destroyed Mariamme, since they believed that if the boys came to power
9   they would pay the penalty for their crimes against their
mother; and this fear became the ground of slanderous
gossip against the boys. They spread the rumour that,
because of their mother's death, they took no pleasure in
their father's company, and considered it an impiety to
10   consort with her murderer, and by making these charges,
to which the facts lent an air of plausibility, they were able
to damage the boys and destroy Herod's affection for
them. They did not speak to him face to face, but spread
their stories among the people at large, and as these were
reported to him they slowly built up a hatred which in
time became too strong for nature itself to control.

11   For the present, however, the king's love for his sons
outweighed all suspicion and calumny, and he gave them
the honour due to them and, when they came of age,
found them wives. To Aristobulus he gave in marriage
Salome's daughter Berenice, and to Alexander the daughter of Archelaus, king of Cappadocia, whose name was
Glaphyra.

12   After making these arrangements he learned that Marcus Agrippa had again sailed from Italy to Asia and made
haste to meet him, inviting him to visit his kingdom and
enjoy the hospitality that he owed him as his friend.
13   Agrippa yielded to his insistence and arrived in Judaea,
where Herod missed no opportunity to please him. He
welcomed him in his newly founded cities, showing him
the buildings and entertaining his party with the most
sumptuous feasts, both in Sebaste and Caesarea, at the
harbour built by him, and also in the fortresses which he
had constructed at great expense, Alexandreion, Herodeion and Hyrcania.

14   He also brought him to the city of Jerusalem, where the
entire population met the great man in festal attire and
cheered him on his arrival. Agrippa sacrificed a hecatomb
15   to God and feasted the people, whose numbers rivalled
those of the greatest cities, and such was his pleasure in

the visit that he would have stayed some days longer. But the time of year, with winter approaching, made his departure a matter of urgency, as he was obliged to return to Ionia and thought that it would be unsafe to delay the voyage.

16 Agrippa therefore sailed away, after Herod had honoured him and the most distinguished of his party with numerous gifts. The king spent the winter at home, but in the spring moved quickly to rejoin him, knowing that he was to lead a campaign to the Bosphorus. Sailing between Rhodes and

17 Cos, he made for shore near Lesbos, thinking that he would overtake Agrippa there, but a north wind caught him there and prevented his ships from putting out. He

18 then spent several days in Chios, welcoming his many visitors and winning their friendship with royal gifts; and on seeing the ruined condition of the city's portico, which had been demolished in the Mithridatic war and, unlike the other buildings, was not easy to restore because of its

19 size and beauty, he made a gift of money which was not merely adequate but more than enough to cover the cost of rebuilding it. And he gave instructions that the work should be done without delay and the portico raised with all speed, so as to restore the city to its former beauty.

20 When the wind had died down, he himself sailed to Mytilene and from there to Byzantium, and on hearing that Agrippa had already sailed into the Black Sea he followed him at full speed. When he finally overtook him

21 at Sinope in Pontus, the sight of Herod as he sailed towards their ships was unexpected, but his appearance was welcomed and they greeted each other warmly.

Agrippa believed that he had the surest proof of the king's loyalty and affection towards him in the long voyage he had completed and the service that he unfailingly rendered to him, a duty to which he gave priority over the management of his own affairs and for which he

22 had left his kingdom. Herod was indeed all in all to him in the campaign, his fellow combatant in affairs of state, his adviser as occasion demanded, and an agreeable companion in moments of relaxation. Herod alone shared his every experience: his troubles by reason of his loyalty, and his pleasures as a mark of respect.

23   When they had completed the business in Pontus on which Agrippa had been sent, they decided not to return by sea, but passed through Paphlagonia and Cappadocia, and travelling overland from there to Great Phrygia, they reached Ephesus, from where they sailed across again to

24 Samos. In every city the king made numerous benefactions according to the needs of his petitioners, unstinting in providing money or hospitality and meeting the expenses himself; and for some of those who asked favours of Agrippa he acted as mediator, ensuring the success of their suits.

25   Agrippa was himself a man of kind and magnanimous disposition, ready to further the interests of those who applied to him so long as no one else was damaged, but

26 willing as he was, it was the influence of the king that especially spurred him to acts of generosity. It was Herod, for example, who reconciled him with the people of Ilium, with whom he had been displeased, while for the Chians he paid the revenue owed to Caesar's procurators and discharged them of their tribute; and he gave assistance to others in accordance with their various requests.

Herod Champions the Jews of Asia

27 It was at this time, while they were in Ionia, that a large number of the Jews who inhabited the cities there took advantage of the opportunity to approach them and speak frankly of the abuses that they were suffering. They complained that they were forbidden to observe their own laws, insulted by the judges by being forced to appear in

28 court on holy days, and deprived of the monies which they intended to send as offerings to Jerusalem. They also said that they were forced to take part in military service and the performance of civic duties and spend their holy offerings on these, in spite of the exemption granted them by the Romans, who had always permitted them to live according to their own laws.

29   As they were making these protests, the king persuaded Agrippa to hear them plead their cause, and assigned Nicolas, one of his own friends, to speak on behalf of

30 their rights. And when Agrippa had appointed the Roman

officials and such kings and princes as were present to be
his assessors, Nicolas stood up and spoke as follows on
behalf of the Jews.

31   All men in their hour of need, most mighty Agrippa, must
have recourse to those with power to remove their grievances; but your present petitioners come with assurance
32   also. You have often fulfilled their wishes in the past, and
they ask only not to be robbed, with your consent, of
privileges granted by yourselves – privileges received from
the only authority empowered to give them, and taken
away not by a superior power but by people whom they
know to be equally your subjects.

33   And indeed, if they have been highly favoured, it is to
their credit that they showed themselves worthy of so much,
while as for small concessions, it would be disgraceful for
those who granted them not also to secure them. Those
34   who obstruct the Jews and use them despitefully are patently guilty of injustice against both parties: they wrong the
recipients of these favours by disregarding their rulers'
testimony to their virtue, and they wrong the donors by
35   seeking the annulment of their concessions. If *they* were
asked which they would rather lose, their lives or their
national customs, such as the processions, sacrifices and
festivals which they celebrate in honour of the gods of their
faith, I am sure that they would prefer any suffering to the
least violation of their traditions.

36   Most men, after all, go to war in defence of these, so
concerned are they not to betray them; and we measure
happiness itself, which all mankind enjoys today on your
account, by the freedom of every nation in its own country
to live and flourish in the observance of its own traditions.
37   So what they would never agree to endure themselves they
seek to impose forcibly on others, as if to destroy the sacred
traditions of any people were not an act of impiety just as
serious as to neglect the worship of their own gods.

38   Let us now consider this further question. Is there any
people or city or nation in the world for whom the protection of your empire and the might of Rome have not proved
the greatest of blessings? And would any wish to cancel the
privileges which they owe to you? No one, not even a

39   madman; for there is no one without a share in them,
whether as a private individual or as a member of his
community. And certainly, those who would deprive others
of favours granted by you forfeit their own right to retain
40   your concessions to them. Yet the privileges they enjoy are
inestimable, for if they were to compare the empire of today
with the monarchies of the past they would find their
happiness increased in many ways, and in one above all,
that they are slaves no longer, but free people.

41   It is true that we Jews are generously favoured, but our
circumstances should not provoke envy, as we owe our
good fortune to you and share it with all men. One thing
only have we asked, the right to uphold without hindrance
the religion of our fathers, a concession which offers no
grounds for resentment and might be thought to be in the
42   interests of those who grant it: for if the Godhead delights
in being honoured, it delights in those who permit it to be
honoured.

Our customs contain no trace of inhumanity, but all tend
towards piety and are hallowed with saving righteousness.
43   We make no secret of the precepts that we use to guide our
lives, whether in our worship or in our dealings with
mankind; and every seventh day we set aside for the study
of our customs and the Law, as we think it right to prepare
ourselves for the avoidance of sin as for any other accom-
44   plishment. These customs will bear scrutiny: they are noble
in themselves and – though some may dispute it – our
ancient inheritance; we have received them and preserve
them as a sacred gift, hallowed by time, and cannot easily
unlearn them.

45   These are the customs which they deny to us, in defiance
of justice, when they seize the monies which we consecrate
to God, and openly steal them from our Temple, when they
impose taxes on us, and when they make us go to court or
conduct other business on holy days. These impositions,
which no contractual obligation sanctions, are an insult to
our religion, against which they have conceived an unjustified and unwarranted hatred; and they know this as well as
we do.

46   Your empire holds all nations under a single sovereignty,
inspiring loyalty and rendering resentment idle for those

47   who prefer the present to the former dispensation. Our
plea, therefore, mighty Agrippa, is this: not to be mistreated
or abused, not to be prevented from observing our own
customs, not to be deprived of our property, and not to
suffer impositions from those whose freedom we ourselves
respect.

48   These requests are not only just, but they were formerly
granted by you, and there are many relevant decrees of the
Senate and tablets laid up in the Capitol that we could read
to you, which were evidently granted after we had proved
our loyalty to you, and which would be valid even if you

49   had favoured us in the absence of such proof. It is not only
we but virtually all mankind whom you have benefited by
your rule, in protecting their existing rights and augmenting
them beyond their hopes, and to rehearse the advantages
which each separate nation owes to you would take an
endless speech.

50   But to make clear that all our own privileges were
rightfully obtained, we will say nothing of the past. It is
enough if we support our claims by reference to our present

51   king, who sits beside you. Has he ever failed to show
friendship to your house? Has he ever been disloyal? Is
there any mark of honour that he has neglected? Is there
any emergency in which he has not shown foresight? And
in that case, what is there to prevent your matching his acts
of goodwill with the number of your favours?

52   It is perhaps also appropriate to make mention of the
valour of his father Antipater, who came to Caesar's aid
with two thousand heavy-armed infantry when he invaded
Egypt, and proved second to none in battle both on land

53   and at sea. What need is there to tell how decisive was their
intervention at that moment, or to recount the many gifts
with which they were severally honoured by Caesar? Yet I
must recall the dispatch which Caesar wrote to the Senate
on that occasion, and the public honours and gifts of
citizenship that Antipater received, since these will be suf-

54   ficient proof that we are entitled to the favours that we
enjoy and to seek from you confirmation of them.

Even if they had not been granted earlier, we might have
expected such favours from you, Agrippa, in view of the

55   mutual goodwill that exists between you and our king. We

are assured by the Jews in Judaea that you entered their
country as a friend, that you offered due sacrifices to God
and honoured Him with fitting prayers, and that you
feasted the people and received their gifts of hospitality in
56   return. From a man of your wide powers all these acts of
kindness to the nation and the city must be accounted
pledges and tokens of the friendship which you have
granted the Jewish nation on the commendation of Herod's
57   own household. In reminding you of them and of our king,
now present at your side, we are making no unreasonable
demand, but merely that you will not allow the rights that
you yourselves have granted to be removed by others.

58   The Greeks made no attempt to refute these points
made by Nicolas, as the Jewish case was not an argument
about specific issues as in a court of law, but a general
59   plea against acts of violence. Their opponents did not deny
what they had done, but claimed in justification that the
Jewish occupation of their land was itself an injustice. The
Jews, however, showed that they were native to the
country and that in honouring their own customs they
were doing no harm in living there.

60   Agrippa realised that they were the victims of oppres-
sion, and therefore replied that, while Herod's goodwill
and friendship to him made him disposed to grant the
Jews any favour they wanted, their petition seemed just in
itself, and even if they had asked for more he would not
have hesitated to give it, so long as Roman authority was
not impaired. But as they had asked no more than that
their former privileges should not be annulled, he confirmed their right to continue living without interference
in the observance of their own customs.

61   With these words he dismissed the meeting, and Herod
came forward and embraced him in grateful acknowledgement of his consideration for him. Agrippa returned the
friendly gesture, putting his arms around Herod and
62   embracing him in the same way. He then departed for
Lesbos. The king, who decided to sail home from Lesbos,
took his leave of Agrippa and put out to sea, and as the
winds were favourable he landed at Caesarea a few days
later.

63 From there he went to Jerusalem and summoned an assembly of the entire population of the city, which was also attended by many people from the countryside. Standing. before them he gave an account of his whole journey abroad, explaining the circumstances of the Asiatic Jews and telling them that on his account they would be free of

64 interference in future. And in general he expressed his pride in his successes and his administration of the kingdom, assuring them that he had neglected nothing that might be to their advantage, and remitted to them one-

65 quarter of their taxes for the past year. The speech and this act of generosity won the hearts of the crowd, who went away delighted, wishing the king all manner of blessings.

Antipater Arrives at Court

66 The dissension in Herod's household continued to grow worse, and a more serious crisis developed. Salome had inherited a hatred of Mariamme's young sons, and employed every stratagem that had succeeded against their mother in a bold and reckless campaign to ensure that none of Mariamme's children might survive to avenge the death of the woman she had destroyed. And the young

67 men for their part displayed a degree of presumption and harboured a grudge against their father, both because they remembered their mother's undeserved fate and because

68 they were ambitious for power. Relations became as bad as ever, with the youths reviling Salome and Pheroras while the other two pursued their malicious purpose against the young men with calculated treachery.

69 On both sides the hatred was the same, but it expressed itself in different ways. The king's sons were quick to abuse and vilify their opponents publicly, in the naïve belief that unrestrained anger was a mark of nobility; whereas Salome and Pheroras, by contrast, had deliberate recourse to malicious gossip, leading the boys on all the time and reckoning that their headstrong behaviour would

70 end in violence against their father. Feeling no shame at their mother's faults and refusing to accept that she had had justice, they were unlikely to stop short of taking

vengeance with their own hands on the man they held responsible.

71   Eventually the whole city was talking of their rivalry, and while there was sympathy for the inexperience of the youths, as in any contest, it was Salome's careful strategy that prevailed. She had no need to tell lies, as they themselves provided the grounds for her accusations. So discon-

72   solate were they over their mother's death that when Salome spoke ill of her and of themselves they would protest indignantly that their mother's downfall was a tragedy – as indeed it was, and that their own position was pitiful, as they were forced to live with her murderers and share the same fate.

73   The situation grew worse when the king's absence abroad put their relationship under further strain; and when Herod returned and addressed the people, as we have described, he was at once assailed by Pheroras and Salome with warnings that he was in great danger from the youths, who were openly threatening that they would not leave their mother's murder unavenged. They also told

74   him that the young men rested their hopes on Archelaus of Cappadocia, intending with his help to gain access to Caesar and bring charges against their father.

75   Herod was shocked at the time by what they said, and became still more dismayed to receive the same report from others. He reviewed the course of his misfortunes, reflecting that in the past he had derived no happiness from those dearest to him and from the wife he had adored, because of the dissensions in his household, and anticipating even greater misery in the future than he had

76   already suffered; and his heart was troubled. It was indeed true that in public affairs heaven had blessed him with the greatest good fortune, beyond all his hopes, yet in his domestic life his expectations of happiness had been griev-

77   ously disappointed. This striking contrast in his fortunes eventually became so marked as to raise the question whether he ought to purchase such success in public life at the cost of domestic unhappiness, when he might have avoided the tragedies that his household suffered by for-going the remarkable achievements of his kingship.

78   In this disturbed state of mind he sent for another of his

sons, named Antipater, who had been born when he was a commoner, with the intention of raising him to a position of honour and thereby weakening the two youths. It was only later that he became wholly dependent on
79 Antipater and let him have his way in everything; for the present, he envisaged no more than making use of him to dent the confidence of Mariamme's sons and serve as a warning to them. Their self-assurance would soon evaporate, he believed, if they were made to realise that they had no sole and undisputed right to the succession.

80 So he introduced Antipater in the role of substitute, believing that he was doing right to take precautions and that, if the youths were checked, he would find them more amenable when the time came to deal with them. But
81 the plan was a failure. The boys considered themselves insulted and unfairly treated, while Antipater, a man of formidable character who had acquired a certain assurance where once he had been without hope, became single-minded in his aim of wrecking his brothers' chances and denying them the pre-eminence. To this end he resolved to continue working on his father, already prejudiced by slander and predisposed to fall in with his purpose, and harden his attitude still more to the victims of that slander.

82 Antipater was not the only source of gossip, as he was careful not to be thought a backbiter. He preferred to use as accomplices men who aroused no suspicion, and who would be trusted as acting purely out of loyalty to the
83 king; and they volunteered their services in increasing numbers, allying themselves with his ambitions and leading Herod on under the pretence of giving information with his best interests at heart. They worked together as a team, acting their many parts with an air of sincerity; but
84 most of their material was supplied by the young men, who would often weep over the insult and indignity they were subjected to, invoking their mother's name and openly seeking to convict their father of injustice in the presence of their friends. Their every show of disaffection was remembered by Antipater and his friends for their own sinister purpose, and reported in exaggerated terms to Herod – all of which went to heighten the tension in the household.

85   Exasperated by the slanders and wishing to humiliate Mariamme's sons, the king virtually always gave the precedence to Antipater, and finally deferred to him so far as to introduce his mother to the palace. He also wrote of him frequently to Caesar, with the warmest personal

86   commendations. Indeed, when Agrippa returned to Rome after his ten years in charge of Asia, Herod sailed from Judaea to meet him with Antipater as his sole companion, and presented him to Agrippa to take to Rome, bearing many gifts, to make the friendship of Caesar. It now seemed that Antipater had unchallenged authority and that the two youths were completely excluded from power.

87   Antipater's residence abroad seemed to enhance his reputation and confirm his pre-eminence. He was a celeb-

88   rity in Rome, as Herod had written of him to all his friends. Yet he was uneasy to be away from home, without the opportunity to continue to discredit his brothers, and was particularly anxious in case his father should change his mind and, left to himself, find reason to take a more favourable view of Mariamme's sons.

89   Brooding on these thoughts, he never rested from his purpose. Even from Rome he regularly wrote to his father with any story that might displease him and rouse his anger against his brothers. He professed himself deeply concerned about his father's safety, but in reality it was his characteristic malice at work, trading on the great hope

90   that he already entertained. In the end he excited such anger and resentment in Herod that he came to see the youths as enemies, while still hesitating to give way to such a feeling. Wishing to avoid a mistake, whether by being too remiss or too precipitate, he thought it better to take ship for Rome, and there accuse his sons before Caesar rather than take the initiative himself, as such a serious violation of family loyalty would lay him open to suspicion.

Herod Accuses Mariamme's Sons to Caesar

91 Herod came to Rome,* therefore, and proceeded to the city of Aquileia in his urgent desire to meet Caesar; and

when granted an audience he requested the opportunity to speak of the great difficulties in which he found himself.

92   Then, bringing forward his sons, he accused them of a desperate conspiracy. Describing them as enemies whose hatred of their own father knew no bounds, he charged them with plotting his destruction and the seizure of his throne by the most monstrous of crimes – and that when he had Caesar's authority to exercise his own free judgement in bequeathing it to the son who proved most loyal

93   to him. Yet their chief concern, he said, was not with power – it mattered little to them to be deprived of this and of life itself, if only they could kill their father, so savage and unholy was the hatred that filled their hearts. This misfortune, which he had long endured in private, he was now compelled to lay before Caesar, and pollute his ears with the story.

94   And yet, he demanded, what harsh treatment had they suffered at his hands? What cruelty could they complain of? And how could it be right, when he had won his kingdom at great personal risk and hardship, that he should be denied his right to own it, to govern it and to

95   dispose of it to a worthy heir? This, of all the prizes that he had to offer for filial piety, was reserved for that son whose consideration for his father would merit such a

96   recompense. But it was plainly no mark of such piety that they should meddle in the matter. A son who forever dreams of becoming king, he argued, must be contemplating the essential precondition of his succession – his father's death.

97   For his own part, he had not failed to that day to give them everything appropriate to a king's subjects and sons, whether a fine wardrobe, or servants, or luxuries. He had also arranged the most illustrious marriages for them, giving his own sister's daughter to Aristobulus and King Archelaus's daughter to Alexander.

98   But above all, when he might have used his authority to punish them for their crimes, he had brought them to Caesar, their common benefactor. He had relinquished all his rights as a father and a king against disloyal and treacherous sons, and awaited judgement as their equal.

99   He would only ask not to go entirely unavenged nor have

to spend his life in the grip of fear. And in view of what his sons had planned, he doubted that it would profit them to see the light of day, even if they should escape on this occasion. They were guilty of the greatest crimes known to man, and their punishment would be proportionate.

100 Such were the heartfelt words with which Herod accused his sons before Caesar. Even as he spoke the young men's distress gave way to tears, but when he finished his speech their confusion deepened. They felt assured in their own consciences that they were innocent

101 of such filial impiety, but they knew very well that it was difficult to defend themselves when the charges were made by their father. It did not seem right for them to speak their minds as the occasion required, if they were going to convict him of violent, precipitate and unreasonable

102 behaviour, and so they were at a loss for words, and their tears turned to deep and heart-rending sobs.

They were afraid that if they stayed silent their failure to respond would be taken as an admission of guilt, but immature and confused as they were, they could find no

103 words to defend themselves. Caesar, however, observed their reaction very carefully and realised that their reluctance was due, not to any consciousness of unnatural crimes, but to inexperience and diffidence. And they evoked the pity of the entire company, and particularly of their father, who was overcome with genuine emotion.

104 They became aware that both Herod and Caesar felt a degree of sympathy for them, and that the others all shared their distress, and some their tears; and Alexander, acting as spokesman, then addressed his father in an attempt to dismiss the charges.

105 Father, your goodwill to us is obvious even on the occasion of this trial, for had you intended to deal severely with us, you would not have brought us before the saviour of all

106 mankind. You possess the authority of a king and of a father to punish the guilty, but your bringing us to Rome to testify to Caesar was designed for our salvation. No one brings a man to a sanctuary or temple if he intends to kill him.

107 But our position is now so much the worse, for we could

not bear to go on living if we were believed to have wronged such a father. It may well be that to live under suspicion of guilt is worse than to die in innocence. So if our honest words are accepted as the truth, we shall be happy to have convinced you and escaped punishment. But if this slander prevails, then we have no more need of the light of day – how could we look at it when under such suspicion?

To impute to young men a desire to be king is a plausible charge, and to make mention of our poor unhappy mother in this context is sufficient to connect the present unhappy episode with the first. Yet consider: is it not generally true that these charges could be made against anyone in such circumstances? Any king with young sons, whose mother has been put to death, will inevitably suspect them all of plotting against their father. But suspicion is not enough, where impiety of this magnitude is alleged. If we have dared to do anything which might lend credence to such incredible charges, then let us hear of it.

Is there any who can convict us of preparing poison, conspiring with our friends, bribing servants, or writing letters against you? Yet every one of these charges, false though they are, has been fabricated by slander. Dissension in a royal household is a terrible thing, and the kingship, which you describe as the prize of loyalty, often rouses ambitions in the worst of men which make their malice throw off all restraint.

No one, then, will prove us guilty of any crime, but as for slanders, they cannot be disposed of unless we are allowed a hearing. Have we spoken freely? Yes – but not against you, which would have been wrong. We have spoken against men who would not hold their tongues even if we had said nothing. Has either of us lamented his mother? Yes – but not because she died, but because even in death she was reviled without reason.

Do we desire the kingly power that we know belongs to our father? To what purpose? If we enjoy royal honours, as we do, would not our labour be in vain? And if not, do we not have hope of them? Could we have expected to gain the throne by killing you, when the earth would not let us tread on it nor the sea let us sail on it after such a deed? Would the piety of your subjects and the whole nation's sense of

religion have allowed parricides to assume the government,
116   and to enter that most holy Temple that you built? And if
we had made light of all other dangers, could a murderer
have escaped punishment while Caesar lives?

Your sons are not so impious or so stupid as this, though
they may be more unlucky than you found convenient. But
117   if you have no ground for accusing us and no evidence of a
plot, what is it that has power to convince you of such
treachery? Our mother is dead but surely her death might
have served to caution us, rather than provoke us.

118   We could say more in our defence, but to address ficti-
tious charges would be a waste of words. Before Caesar,
therefore, the master of the world and our present mediator,
119   we propose this agreement. If you, Father, will rid your
mind of all suspicion towards us, in very truth, then we
shall live. Even so, it will not be a happy life – it is a terrible
120   thing to face so grave a charge, even when the charge is
false. But if any anxiety remains, continue on your blame-
less course, and we will make our own reckoning. Life is
not so precious to us that we would have it at the cost of
wronging the father who gave it to us.

121   Caesar had been sceptical from the start because of the
gravity of the charge, and his support for the youths was
confirmed by Alexander's speech. He kept his eyes on
Herod, noticing that even he was uneasy. Those attending
the hearing looked on in anguish, and a murmur of
resentment against the king ran round the hall. The charge
122   was incredible, and this, together with the sympathy
aroused by young men in the bloom and beauty of youth,
favoured their cause, and the more so because of Alexander's shrewd and thoughtful reply to his father's speech.
Even the young men themselves now cut a different figure,
for though they still wept and looked in dejection at the
ground, a ray of hope could be seen.

123   As for the king, he had persuaded himself that his
accusations were reasonable, but had no means of proving
124   them, and his conduct called for some justification. After
a brief pause, therefore, Caesar said that, while the young
men seemed entirely innocent of the charge against them,
there was one respect in which they were at fault. If they

125 had behaved correctly towards their father they would never have incurred the slander. And he urged Herod to cast aside all suspicion and become reconciled to his sons, saying that it was wrong even to believe such accusations against his own children. He added that this change of heart could not only heal the wounds that both sides had suffered but could also promote a better understanding between them. All that was needed was that they should exchange apologies for their overhasty distrust and resolve to cultivate a more affectionate relationship.

126   With these words of advice he beckoned to the young men, and they would have fallen at their father's feet in supplication. But Herod forestalled them, and as they wept took each boy in his arms in turn with an embrace; and there was no one present, whether freeman or slave, who was not moved at the sight.

127   They then gave thanks to Caesar and went away together accompanied by Antipater, who pretended to be
128 glad they were reconciled. During the days that followed Herod made Caesar a gift of three hundred talents to finance his provision of public shows and doles for the people of Rome, while Caesar gave Herod half the revenue of the copper mines of Cyprus and the management of the other half. He also entertained him as his honoured guest,
129 and gave him authority to appoint the son of his choice as heir to his kingdom, or even to arrange for his sons to share the title. Herod wished to make the settlement at once, but he refused to allow him to relinquish control of his kingdom, or of his sons, during his lifetime.

130   After this Herod returned to Judaea. During his absence abroad a rebellion had occurred in the district of Tracho-
131 nitis, a substantial part of his kingdom, but the generals he had left in charge had suppressed it and forced the people to submit. Accompanied by his sons he put in at the island of Elaeusa near Cilicia, now renamed Sebaste. Here he met Archelaus, king of Cappodocia, who welcomed him warmly, delighted that he was reconciled with his sons, and that Alexander, his son-in-law, had been acquitted of the charge. And in the tradition of royalty they exchanged gifts.

132   Herod then made for Judaea, and on arriving in the

Temple precinct gave an account of his business abroad, mentioning Caesar's kindness to him and such of his own doings as he thought it expedient that the people should

133 know. He concluded his speech by admonishing his sons, and urging the members of his court and the rest of the people to live in harmony. He then nominated his successors to the royal title: first Antipater, and after him Mariamme's sons, Alexander and Aristobulus.

134 But for the present he asked them all to look to him as their king and master. Old age, he said, was no hindrance to him, and was the time of life when experience had most to contribute to the business of government; nor was he deficient in any of the arts of governing a kingdom and ruling his sons. To his officers and soldiers he said that if they owed allegiance to him alone, they would have an untroubled life, and that they and he would have every opportunity to promote each other's happiness.

135 With these words he dismissed the assembly. Most of his audience were pleased by what he had to say, but not all of them. Because of the hopes that he had held out to his sons, rivalry was already making itself felt and there was much discontent and desire for change.

Liberality and Oppression

136 At about this time Herod's building of Caesarea Sebaste was completed. The entire work of construction was finished in the tenth year, as the time allowed for it was extended into the twenty-eighth year of his reign,* in the hundred and ninety-second Olympiad. To celebrate its

137 dedication a great festival was promptly held, for which the most lavish preparations were made. He had announced that there was to be a musical competition and athletic games, and had arranged a large programme of fights between gladiators and wild beasts, together with horse races and the extravagant spectacles that are seen in

138 Rome and elsewhere. These games, like the city, he dedicated to Caesar, and proposed to hold them every four years.* Caesar himself supplied all the equipment needed

139 for them at his own expense, a gesture that enhanced his reputation for munificence, while his wife Julia on her

own account sent from Rome many of her costliest treasures to a total value of at least five hundred talents.

140   A great crowd gathered in the city to see the sights, including official representatives sent by communities in gratitude for Herod's benefits to them; and he welcomed them all, providing board and lodging for them and entertaining them with feasts. In the daytime the festival offered the attraction of the shows, while at night there was merrymaking on so costly a scale that his generosity

141   became renowned. In all his undertakings it was his ambition to surpass in magnificence anything that had been done before, and they say that Caesar himself and Agrippa often observed that Herod's dominions were too limited to do justice to his magnanimity, and that he deserved to be king of all Syria and of Egypt.

142   After this festival and the celebrations were over, Herod built another city in the Plain of Capharsaba,* selecting a well-watered and exceptionally fertile site. The city itself stood in the bend of a river, surrounded by a stately grove of trees, and he called it Antipatris after his father Antipa-

143   ter. Above Jericho he built a stronghold to which he gave his mother's name of Cypros, and which, while remarkable for its security, was furnished with the most agreeable living-quarters. And to his brother Phasael, in token of his

144   love for him, he dedicated the most beautiful of monuments by erecting a tower the height of Pharos in the city itself. He called it Phasael, and while it contributed to the city's defences its name made it also a memorial to his

145   dead brother. He also founded a city named after him further north in the valley of Jericho, and through the good husbandry of the people he settled there he made the surrounding countryside, which was previously a wilderness, more productive. He called this city Phasaelis.

146   I cannot hope to mention all the other benefactions which he bestowed on the cities in Syria and Greece, and wherever he happened to travel. He is reputed to have made himself responsible for the discharge of many civic duties and the construction of public works, and to have donated generous sums of money for the completion of earlier projects on

147   which work had ceased. I will confine myself to the most important and celebrated of his benefactions.

For the people of Rhodes he erected the Pythian temple at his own expense, and made available many talents of silver for shipbuilding. For the people of Nicopolis near Actium, a city founded by Caesar, he helped in the construction of the greater part of their public buildings. For

148 the people of Antioch, the greatest city in Syria, he adorned the broad street which runs the length of the city by building colonnades on either side and paving the open roadway with polished stone, greatly enhancing the beauty of the place as well as serving the convenience of its

149 citizens. And by designating revenues for their maintenance he raised the reputation of the Olympic Games, which had declined for lack of funds and become quite unworthy of their famous name. He gave the festival a new dignity by the provision of sacrifices and other ceremonies, and in recognition of his liberality the people of Elis declared him perpetual president of the games in their inscriptions.

150 Herod's policies were characterised by two distinct tendencies, a fact which has usually caused surprise. On the one hand, when we have regard to his liberality and the benefactions that he made to mankind in general, even his detractors would be forced to admit the remarkable gen-

151 erosity of his nature. Yet when we consider his vengeful and unjustified treatment of his subjects and his closest relatives, and observe the unrelenting harshness of his

152 character, we must regard him as a brute, quite devoid of self-restraint. It is generally thought, for these reasons, that his actions sprang from separate and contradictory motives. But I take a different view and believe that both aspects of his character have the same explanation.

153 Herod loved honour, and was dominated by that passion, and his magnanimity revealed itself wherever

154 there was hope of a lasting memorial or of immediate fame. But he spent beyond his means, and the oppressive nature of his regime was the necessary consequence. His lavish expenditure on the recipients of his bounty made him a source of misery to the people from whom he took

155 the money. Well aware that he was hated for the injustices he inflicted on his subjects, he could see no easy way to redress these wrongs, with the loss of revenue that would

have been entailed; instead, he remained defiant, using their resentment as an excuse to satisfy his wants.

156 If any of his close acquaintance failed to flatter him with professions of servile obedience, or seemed to call his authority in question, he would lose all self-control, and persecute relatives and friends alike with a vengeance appropriate to an enemy in war. These excesses he committed from a desire to be uniquely honoured.

157 To support my contention that this was his overriding motive I can refer to the ways in which he gave honour to Caesar, Agrippa and his other friends. He expected to receive the same deference himself as he showed to his superiors, and in treating this as the most precious gift he

158 had to give he revealed his desire to win similar honours for himself. The Jewish people, however, have been taught by their Law to disdain all such ambition, and to admire righteousness rather than the pursuit of glory. As a result they incurred his displeasure, finding it impossible to flatter the king's ambition with statues, temples and such marks of honour.

159 This, then, seems to me the explanation both of Herod's crimes against his own people and his counsellors and also of his generosity towards foreigners and people unconnected to him.

Here Josephus interrupts his narrative to give the texts of Roman decrees upholding the rights of Jews in Asia and Cyrene.

Herod Opens King David's Tomb

179 Herod, who had spent vast sums both on external needs and on the needs of his own kingdom, had learned some time before how Hyrcanus, one of his predecessors, had opened David's tomb and taken three thousand talents of silver.* There was said to be a much larger treasure still deposited there, enough to defray all his expenses, and he had long entertained the idea of getting his hands on it. This he now proceeded to do.

180 Opening the tomb by night, and taking great care to be

181 unobserved by anyone in the city, he went inside accompanied only by his most trustworthy friends. Unlike Hyrcanus, he found no money stored there, but a wealth of gold ornaments and other treasures, all of which he took away. He was eager to make a more thorough search by
182 going further inside, right up to the coffins containing the bodies of David and Solomon; but two of his bodyguards, so it was said, were struck dead as they entered by a flash of flame, and Herod emerged again overcome with dread. To propitiate the terror he built, at enormous cost, a
183 memorial of white marble at the entrance to the tomb. This monument is mentioned by his contemporary, the historian Nicolas, who nevertheless denies that Herod went down into the tomb, as he knew such behaviour to be improper.
184   This is the policy that Nicolas generally follows in his work. He lived during Herod's reign, as an associate of the king, and therefore wrote to please him and be of service to him. He treats only of the facts that tend to Herod's credit, while excusing or resolutely concealing his
185 notorious injustices. The deaths of Mariamme and her sons, for example, were acts of the grossest cruelty on the king's part, but Nicolas, wishing to present them in a good light, falsely accuses her of sexual misconduct and the young men of treachery. He remains consistent throughout his work, heaping fulsome praise upon the king's just dealings while doing his best to defend his unlawful acts.
186   Nicolas, as I said, may be largely exonerated, as his intention was not to write a history for others but to be of
187 service to the king. We, however, who belong to a family closely related to the Hasmonaean kings which has the priesthood among its honours,* consider it improper to tell lies about them, and offer an honest and fair account of their doings. Many descendants of that line are still in power, and while we respect them we honour the truth even more. Indeed, there have been occasions when fair comment has incurred their anger.

The Domestic Strife Intensifies

188 Herod's violation of the tomb seemed responsible for increasing disarray within his household. It may be that

the wrath of God caused the particular ills from which he suffered to intensify, until the affliction became incurable, or else a stroke of Fortune, coinciding with his guilt, gave strong grounds for believing that his misfortunes were the

189 consequence of impiety. The dissension in the palace was like a civil war, and in their mutual hatred each side sought to cap the slanders of the other.

190 Antipater was always scheming against his brothers, cunningly ensnaring them with accusations brought by others while often taking the opportunity to speak in their defence – this semblance of friendship having the aim of winning trust and assisting his designs against them. He succeeded by these devious methods in getting round his father and convincing him that he, and he alone, was

191 doing all he could for his protection. And Herod recommended Ptolemy, his minister of finance, to Antipater's friendship and consulted with Antipater's mother about urgent matters of state. They had complete authority to do as they liked and to prejudice the king against others whenever they considered it to their own advantage.

192 The position of Mariamme's sons, on the other hand, became increasingly difficult. Because of their noble birth they could not bear the dishonour of being pushed aside

193 and made to occupy a less elevated role. As for the women, Alexander's wife Glaphyra, the daughter of Archelaus, incurred the hatred of Salome both because of the love she felt for her husband and because she treated Salome's daughter, the wife of Aristobulus, with great disdain, indignant at her equality of rank.

194 Now besides this second quarrel that had befallen them, the king's brother Pheroras was also in trouble and giving Herod reasons of his own to feel distrust and bitterness. He had fallen in love with one of his female slaves, and his infatuation with the woman held him captive to such a degree that he scorned the king's daughter,* who was betrothed to him, and set his heart on the slave.

195 Herod was angered at the insult. He had done his brother many favours and given him a share of the royal power, but finding his kindness unrequited he felt that he had made

196 an unfortunate choice. And so, as Pheroras had behaved dishonourably, he gave his daughter to the son of Phasael.*

But some time later, when he believed that his brother's passion had spent its heat, he chided him with his amorous behaviour and asked him to take his second daughter, who was called Cypros. Ptolemy, too, advised Pheroras to abandon his passion now and cease insulting his brother, telling him that the charms of a slave girl were a disgraceful reason to forfeit the king's goodwill and incur his hatred by frustrating his wishes.

197

Pheroras saw that this course of action would be in his interests, as he had been pardoned once before when he was the subject of accusations. He therefore put away the woman, though he already had a child by her, and agreed to marry the king's second daughter, fixing the wedding for thirty days from that time, and swearing an oath to have no further contact with the woman he had put away.

198

However, when the thirty days had passed he was still so mastered by his love that he carried out none of his promises but resumed his relationship with the first woman. Herod was now visibly hurt and angered by his conduct, to which he repeatedly referred in conversation, and there were many who used the king's displeasure as an opportunity to discredit Pheroras.

199

200

Not a day, not one hour went by in which the king's mind was at peace. Among his relatives and closest friends new antagonisms continued to arise. Salome, for example, the bitter enemy of Mariamme's sons, would not even allow her daughter, the wife of Aristobulus, one of the two youths, to honour him as her husband, but prevailed on her to report his private conversations; and when their relationship encountered difficulties, as is liable to happen, she filled her daughter with distrust of him.

201

By these means Salome learned of everything that passed between them and turned her daughter against the young man. And she, to please her mother, would often tell how, when they were alone, the young men spoke regretfully of Mariamme but felt hatred for their father; and how they kept threatening that, if they ever came to power, they would see that Herod's sons by his other wives were made village clerks – an office to which they were well suited, they suggested, in view of the elaborate concern which they were currently showing for their education. She also

202

203

204 told her mother that if they saw any of the women making use of their mother's clothes, they threatened to have them dressed in hairshirts instead of their present finery, and kept in confinement without even a sight of the sun.

205   These remarks were at once reported by Salome to the king, and though it grieved him to hear them he tried to put things right. But suspicion continued to gnaw at him and steadily corrupted him, and he began to believe everyone, no matter who were the victims of their slander. For the present, however, he felt easier after rebuking his sons and hearing their defence. Much more serious troubles were to befall him in the days that followed.

206   It was Pheroras again who was responsible. He came to Alexander, who was married to Glaphyra, Archelaus's daughter, as we have related, and said that he had heard from Salome that Herod had fallen in love with Glaphyra and that his desire for her was implacable. On hearing this

207 Alexander became incensed with a young man's jealousy, and remembering Herod's many acts of kindness to the girl he attributed such marks of respect to a dishonourable

208 motive, his suspicions excited by the allegations. Then, unable to bear the pain that the affair caused him, he went to his father in tears and told him what Pheroras had said.

   Herod was now beside himself with rage, deeply embarrassed and indignant that such a slander should have been

209 invented. Again and again he deplored the wickedness of his family and their failure to requite his kindness to them; and then, sending for Pheroras, he reproached him again.

   'You disgrace to humanity!' he said. 'Is there now no bound or limit to your ingratitude, that you should think

210 such things of me, and say such things? I see your purpose, of course. The tales you told my son were meant as more than slander. This was a plot to destroy me, and you chose words for your poison.

211   'Who would hesitate to take vengeance on his father, suspecting this? Only the guidance of heaven could have stayed my son's hand. Was it just an idea that you put in his mind, do you suppose – or was it a sword in his hand to use against his father? You hate him, and his brother. How can you pretend to be his friend – merely to vilify

me, and speak such slanders as only your impious treachery could conceive?

212   'Get away from me, you traitor to your benefactor and
brother, and may your guilt live with you! As for me, I
hope still to prevail over my family without punishing
them as they deserve, and by showing greater kindness
than they are entitled to expect!'

213   Such were the king's words. Pheroras, caught in the very
act of villainy, said that Salome had put him up to it and

214   that she was the source of the story. But Salome, who was
present, no sooner heard this than she protested, with
apparent sincerity, that she had done nothing of the sort.
They were all bent on making the king hate her, she said,
and on destroying her by any means they could, because
of the affection she felt for Herod and her habit of

215   anticipating the dangers that threatened him. But at the
present moment she believed herself to be the target of a
more determined plot, for she alone was trying to persuade
her brother to put away his wife and marry the king's
daughter, and had naturally incurred his hatred.

216   As she spoke she kept tearing at her hair and beating
her breast, a display that lent her denial some credibility
even while her malevolent nature betrayed the insincerity

217   of her actions. Pheroras was left stranded, having nothing
creditable to say in his defence. He had admitted to telling
the tale, and his claim to have heard it at second-hand was

218   not believed. The disorder increased and the battle of
words became more strident, until finally the king dismissed his brother and sister in disgust. Then, after prais-
ing his son for his self-restraint and for acquainting him
with the allegations, he went at a late hour to take some
rest.

219   This confrontation damaged Salome's reputation, as she
was thought to be responsible for the bitterness caused by
the slander. The king's wives, too, resented her, knowing
her to be a very difficult character and subject to changes
of mood – an enemy one moment and a friend the next.
They always had some complaint against her to mention
to Herod, and what happened next made them even bolder
in speaking their minds.

220   The king of Arabia, Obadas, was an unenterprising and

indolent person whose government was conducted, for the most part, by Syllaeus, a clever man who was still young
221 and handsome. Syllaeus had come to visit Herod on business, and while dining with him saw Salome and set his heart on her. Knowing that she was a widow, he
222 engaged her in conversation. Salome, who was even more out of favour with her brother than formerly, eyed the young man with interest, and the idea of marriage appealed to her.

On the days that followed, when they went to dinner the couple gave many unambiguous signs that an under-
223 standing existed between them, and the other women reported them to the king and scoffed at their lack of propriety. Herod questioned Pheroras about it as well and asked him to observe them during dinner to assess their feelings for each other. He reported that it was obvious from their gestures and their eyes that they were both in love.

224 The Arab, his intentions suspected, subsequently went away, but after two or three months he returned to arrange the matter, and proposed to Herod that he should give him Salome for his wife. In support of his proposal he suggested that the match would not be without profit for Herod by linking him with the government of Arabia, which was already virtually in his hands and due to be his
225 by right. Herod conveyed the proposal to his sister and asked if she was ready for the marriage, and she promptly accepted. But when they asked Syllaeus to be initiated into the Jewish faith, as a necessary precondition of the marriage, he refused, saying that he would be stoned to death by the Arabs if he did so, and took his leave.

226 As a result of this episode, Pheroras now proceeded to accuse Salome of licentious behaviour, and the women
227 went further and said that she had been the Arab's mistress. And she suffered a further slight concerning the girl whom the king had betrothed to his brother but whom Pheroras, as I mentioned, had rejected through his love for the slave woman. Salome requested that the girl be given to her son by Costobarus, and Herod was disposed to
228 make the match but was dissuaded by Pheroras, who said that the young man would not be loyal to him because of

the murder of his father, and that it would be more proper
for his own son to have her, since he would succeed him
as tetrarch. The girl's betrothal was rearranged, therefore,
and she was married to Pheroras's young son, the king
contributing a hundred talents to her dowry.

Herod Conducts an Inquisition

229 But Herod had no respite from the troubles of his household, which became increasingly disarrayed. One such
incident, which arose in sordid circumstances, had
unpleasant and far-reaching consequences. The king had
230 some eunuchs, to whom he was extremely attached
because of their beauty. One used to pour his wine,
another to serve his dinner, while the third put him to bed
and was given responsibility for the most important affairs
231 of state. Someone told the king that they had been corrupted by his son Alexander, who had paid them large
bribes. Herod asked them if they had had sexual intercourse with Alexander, and they confessed that they had,
but said they were aware of no other way in which he had
offended his father.
232   When put to the torture, however, and reduced to the
extremity of pain, as the attendants kept stretching the
rack to oblige Antipater, they said that resentment and
233 hatred of his father was ingrained in Alexander's nature,
and that he had told them that Herod had already lived
too long and despaired of his survival – he was even
dyeing his hair black to disguise his senility and conceal
the evidence of his age. And he had promised them that if
they gave him their allegiance they would have first place
in the kingdom when it came into his hands. No one else
234 had a right to it, he had said, whatever the king's wish,
and power was now his for the taking; it was his birth-
right, and his preparations were made. He had many of
the leading citizens and many friends on his side, men with
the courage to do and to suffer whatever was required.
235   When Herod heard these allegations he was outraged,
and he was also very frightened. The insults infuriated
him, while the intimations of treachery alerted him to
danger. Exasperated and embittered on both accounts, he

was afraid it might be true that there was a conspiracy
236 against him too powerful for him to resist at that moment.
He proceeded to investigate in secret, therefore, sending
spies to watch the people he suspected. Distrusting and
hating everyone alike, and believing a regular policy of
distrust to be necessary to his security, he kept under
237 constant suspicion even those who gave him no cause.
There was no limit to this. Those who were considered his
friends aroused his fears all the more because of their
greater influence, while more distant acquaintances needed
only to be named for their deaths to seem necessary to his
survival.

238   Eventually his courtiers, having no assurance of their
own safety, turned on each other, each supposing that he
could save himself by pre-emptive slandering of the others.
But if they succeeded in their bids they became the target
of jealousy, their only achievement being to suffer themselves, and with good reason, the fate they had wrongly
239 contrived for others. Some of them, in fact, were now
pursuing private quarrels in this manner, but when they
were caught they found themselves in the same trap. They
had seen the crisis as an opportunity to ensnare their
enemies, but were caught by the very stratagem which
240 they had devised for others. For the king soon came to
regret having killed people who were guilty of no obvious
crime, and the dire consequence was that, rather than put
an end to the killing, he took the same vengeance on the
informers.

241   While the court was in such turmoil, the king went so far
as to forbid many of his friends to appear before him in
future or enter the palace, an injunction he issued to escape
242 the restriction and embarrassment that their presence
caused him. Andromachus and Gemellus, for example,
were men who had long been his friends and had given
valuable service to his house in matters of state as ambassadors and advisers, and had also helped to educate his
sons. They had been free to speak their minds as no others,
243 but he now dismissed them, Andromachus because his son
Demetrius was a regular companion of Alexander, and
Gemellus because he knew him to be on good terms with
his son, as they had been brought up and educated together

and spent time together when Alexander was in Rome. Herod would gladly have consigned them to a worse fate, but against men of their distinction he was not at liberty to go so far, and confined himself to depriving them of their rank and of the power to prevent his own excesses.

244   The cause of all this was Antipater. He had long been a counsellor of Herod, and when he observed his father's morbid lack of restraint he used his influence with him in the hope of strengthening his own position by quietly eliminating everyone who had the power to oppose him. It

245   was when Andromachus and his friends had been debarred from speaking their minds that the king first questioned under torture everyone he believed to owe allegiance to Alexander, to discover if they knew that a coup had been planned against him; but they died with nothing to tell him.

246   Herod, however, became all the more determined when he failed to bring the suspected plot to light, and Antipater exploited the situation cleverly by accusing the innocent of obduracy and of loyalty to Alexander, and urging Herod to extend his enquiry to uncover the secret plot.

247   Among the many victims of torture there was one who said that he knew of many occasions when the young man had been praised for his physique, or his accuracy with the

248   bow, and for the other qualities in which he had no equal, and had replied that these gifts of nature were not a blessing but a curse, as his father envied and resented them. When he walked with his father, Alexander had said, he would crouch and stoop so as not to appear the taller, and when hunting with him he would shoot wide of the mark, knowing his father's ambition to excel in these accomplishments.

249   While his statement was being examined and his body allowed some relief, he added that Alexander, with Aristobulus as his accomplice, had plotted to ambush and kill his father on a hunting expedition, and when the deed was done to make off to Rome to lay claim to the throne. A

250   letter was also discovered from the young man to his brother, in which he complained of his father's unfairness in assigning land to Antipater that brought in revenue of two hundred talents.

251   Herod's immediate reaction to this evidence was to see it

as confirming his suspicion of his sons, and he arrested and
imprisoned Alexander. But he continued with his ruthless
inquisition, partly because he was not wholly convinced by
what he had heard. On thinking it over he could recall
nothing in their behaviour that indicated a plot, but only
complaints and youthful rivalry, and he thought it unlikely
that, after killing him, Alexander should openly set off for
252 Rome. He thought it right, therefore, to get stronger proof
of his son's treachery, and was determined not to be judged
overhasty for condemning him to imprisonment.

He proceeded to torture those of Alexander's friends
who held positions of authority, putting not a few of them
to death, but they gave him none of the information he was
253 looking for. However, his obsessive search continued, while
fear and confusion held sway in the palace, until one of the
younger men, in the extremity of pain, said that Alexander
had sent a message to his friends in Rome, asking them to
have Caesar summon him at once, as he had information
of a plot against him – his father had made an alliance
against the Romans with Mithridates, the king of Parthia.
And he added that Alexander had poison prepared in
Ascalon.

254 Herod believed this story, feeling flattered that the news
was worse than he anticipated and taking comfort in his
troubles from the thought that his precipitate behaviour
had been vindicated. He at once had a thorough search
made for the drug, but it could not be found. Grave as the
255 situation was, Alexander was in a contentious mood and
ready to make it worse, and instead of denying the charges
he countered his father's summary punishment by a still
greater crime. It may be that his intention was to shame his
father for his readiness to believe slander, but his principal
aim was to damage Herod and the whole kingdom – if his
story were believed.

256 He wrote a statement in four parts and sent it out, saying
that there was no need for torture or further investigation,
since there had been a plot and his accomplices had been
Pheroras and the most trusted of the king's friends. He also
claimed that Salome had entered his room one night and
257 forced him to have intercourse with her. And he said that
everyone was now of one mind, to get rid of Herod

immediately and so be free of their continual anxiety. Ptolemy and Sapinnius, the king's most faithful friends, were among those accused.

258   In what can only be described as a fit of madness, men who had formerly been close friends began to attack each other like wild beasts. Having no opportunity to defend themselves or to rebut slander with the truth, all alike were under constant threat of death without a trial. Some bewailed their own imprisonment or impending death, while others grieved in anticipation of similar fates. A melancholy silence filled the palace, where once there had

259   been happiness. Herod was distraught and felt his whole life a burden to him, distrusting everyone and sorely tormented by his own anxiety. Many times he fancied that he

260   saw his son advancing on him or standing over him with a sword, and he brooded on this thought night and day, displaying symptoms of madness or imbecility. Such was the state to which he was reduced.

Archelaus Acts as Mediator

261   When Archelaus, the king of Cappadocia, learned of Herod's activities, he was worried for his daughter and her young husband, and concerned that a man who was his friend should be so distressed; and so he came to Judaea to show how seriously he viewed the matter.

262   Finding the state the king was in, he decided that to reproach him or suggest that he had acted rashly would be extremely undiplomatic in the circumstances – Herod would become quarrelsome if he were criticised, and the more he strove to defend himself the angrier he would become.

263   Archelaus therefore pursued a different approach towards setting right the unhappy state of the palace. He expressed anger against the young man, and told Herod that he had been considerate in avoiding any precipitate action; and he promised to dissolve his daughter's marriage to Alexander and spare not even her, if she knew of her husband's guilt and had failed to inform Herod.

264   Archelaus's attitude came as a surprise to Herod, the

display of anger tending to justify his conduct, and the king began to soften. Now that he was assured that he had acted fairly, feelings of fatherly concern slowly took
265 the place of bitterness. But he was a pathetic figure in either state. On the one hand, he flew into a rage if anyone tried to refute the slanders against his son; yet when Archelaus lent his weight to the accusations, he was moved to tears of the most affecting grief, begging the other not to dissolve the marriage, nor to feel such anger over the young man's misdeeds.

266 Finding him more reasonable, Archelaus now shifted the charges to the king's friends, saying that it was they who were responsible for corrupting Alexander, a young man innocent of malice, and pointed the finger of suspicion at Herod's brother.

267 Pheroras was already out of favour with Herod, and as he had no one else to effect a reconciliation and saw that Archelaus had the most influence with the king, he made a personal appeal to him, wearing the black garb of mourning and all the marks of impending doom. Without
268 dismissing his plea, Archelaus replied that in view of the king's mood he was powerless to change his mind immediately, and that it would be better for Pheroras to go to him, confess that he was to blame for everything, and beg for his mercy. This, he said, would appease Herod's violent mood, and he promised to be there himself to give his support.

269 Pheroras did as he suggested, and both purposes were accomplished: the charges against Alexander were unexpectedly dismissed, and Archelaus reconciled Pheroras with Herod. He then left for Cappadocia, having won himself a unique place in Herod's favour at that critical time. In recognition of this Herod honoured him with the most lavish gifts, and showed by other splendid tributes that he considered him one of the most valued of his
270 friends. He also made an agreement to go to Rome, since Caesar had been sent an account of this affair, and they travelled together as far as Antioch. Here Herod made the peace between Archelaus and Titius, governor of Syria, who had been at odds with him after a quarrel. He then returned to Judaea.

Herod's Arab Campaign Incurs the Displeasure of Augustus

271 After he had been to Rome and returned again, war broke out between Herod and the Arabs. The cause was as follows. The inhabitants of Trachonitis, the district which Caesar had taken from Zenodorus and added to Herod's dominions, no longer had licence to engage in banditry, but
272 were forced to till the land and live at peace, an uncongenial existence which produced scant reward for their labours. Nevertheless, they refrained for a time from robbing their neighbours, because of the king's ban, and Herod as a result acquired a great reputation for efficient government.
273 But after he sailed to Rome, on the occasion when he brought charges against his son Alexander and personally commended his son Antipater to Caesar's protection, the people of Trachonitis spread the rumour that he was dead, and rebelled against his rule and resumed their traditional
274 habit of robbing their neighbours. At the time, the king's generals put them down in his absence; but some forty ringleaders, frightened by the reprisals taken against the
275 captives, fled the country and made for Arabia, where they were welcomed by Syllaeus, the disappointed suitor of Salome. Syllaeus gave them a stronghold to occupy, and, based in his territory with licence to continue their depredations, their marauding bands overran not only Judaea but all of Coele-Syria too.
276 Returning from Rome to find widespread damage done to his dominions, Herod was unable to get hold of the robbers because of the security they enjoyed under the protection of the Arabs, but he took stern retribution for their crimes by surrounding Trachonitis and slaughtering
277 their kinsmen. The Arabs were enraged by his action, and their law demands vengeance at any cost on those who slay their kinsmen. As a result they now began a continuous campaign of plunder over Herod's entire kingdom, reckless of the consequences.
In discussions with Caesar's governors, Saturninus and Volumnius,* Herod requested that the bandits be delivered
278 to him for punishment, but as their strength increased and their numbers grew, they spread confusion everywhere in

an attempt to devastate his kingdom, sacking towns and villages and slaughtering their captives. By this time they
279 numbered about a thousand, and their incursions resembled all-out war. Herod in exasperation demanded the surrender of the bandits, and also insisted on recovering a loan of sixty talents which Syllaeus had negotiated for Obadas, since the date fixed for its repayment had passed.

280 Syllaeus, however, who had usurped Obadas's power and taken sole charge of affairs, emphatically denied that the bandits were in Arabia and deferred the payment of the money. After discussion of these matters before Saturninus and Volumnius, the governors of Syria, it was finally agreed
281 with Roman arbitration that within thirty days Herod's loan should be repaid, and both sides should surrender any enemy refugees who were in their kingdoms. In the event, not a single Arab was found under Herod's protection, whether to escape justice or for any other reason, whereas the Arabs were convicted of sheltering the bandits.

282 When the appointed time expired, Syllaeus, who had fulfilled none of his obligations, left for Rome. Herod now took steps to enforce the repayment of the debt and the surrender of the bandits protected by the Arabs, and when
283 Saturninus and Volumnius gave him permission to proceed against them for not honouring the agreement, he led his army into Arabia, completing a seven days' march in only three days. Arriving at the fortress which held the bandits, he stormed it and took them all captive. This stronghold, which was called Rhaepta, he then razed to the ground, but did no other damage.

284 The Arabs, however, under the command of Nakebos, mounted a counter-attack, and a battle ensued in which Herod's losses were few, while Nakebos and about twenty-five of his men fell on the enemy side, the rest
285 taking to flight. After punishing the Arabs, Herod settled three thousand Idumaeans in Trachonitis to curb the activities of the bandits there, and sent to the Roman governors, who were in Phoenicia, a report of these exploits, explaining that he had done no more than was necessary to punish the Arabs for their default. The Romans investigated his claims thoroughly and found them to be accurate.

286   However, messengers sped to Syllaeus in Rome and gave
       him a full account of events in which, as might be expected,
287 every detail was exaggerated. Syllaeus had already con-
       trived to make himself known to Caesar and was in atten-
       dance at court at the time. On hearing their report, he at
       once dressed himself in black and appeared before Caesar
       to tell him that Arabia had been devastated by war, his
       whole kingdom laid waste, and that Herod's army was
288 reponsible for the pillage. Tearfully he went on to say that
       two thousand five hundred Arabs of high rank had been
       killed; that their commander Nakebos, his friend and kins-
       man, was among the dead; that the wealth deposited in
       Rhaepta had been taken for plunder; and that Obadas had
       not had the strength to sustain a war and had been treated
289 with contempt, because of his own absence and that of the
       Arab army. To these remarks Syllaeus added invidiously
       that he would not have left his country if he had not been
       assured of Caesar's concern that they should all live in
       peace together, and that if he had been there he would not
       have allowed Herod to profit from the war.
            Stung by his words, Caesar had one question only for
       Herod's representatives and for his own informants who
       had come from Syria: had Herod led his army beyond his
290 borders? They were required to answer this simple ques-
       tion without having a chance to explain Herod's reasons
       or his conduct of the campaign, and Caesar's temper
       worsened. He wrote Herod a stern letter, the main thrust
       of which was that, whereas he had formerly treated him
       as a friend, he would now treat him as a subject.
291 Syllaeus, too, wrote to the Arabs about what had hap-
       pened, and excited by the news they refused to surrender
       any of the bandits who had taken refuge with them or to
       repay their debts, and withheld the rent for pastures which
       they occupied as tenants of Herod. The king of the Jews,
       they had heard, had been humiliated and felt the wrath of
292 Caesar! The people of Trachonitis also seized the oppor-
       tunity to revolt against their Idumaean garrison and take
       to banditry; and in this they were joined by the Arabs,
       who ravaged the Idumaeans' lands all the more fiercely to
       settle scores as well as make a profit.
293   All this Herod had to endure. He had lost the assurance

that he owed to Caesar's friendship, and his spirits were low. Even when he sent an embassy to plead his cause, Caesar declined to receive them, and sent them away with nothing accomplished. Dejected and apprehensive at the turn of events, he was sorely tried by the fact that Syllaeus, who had the confidence of Caesar, was present in Rome – indeed, he was at that moment aspiring to even greater power.

294

Obadas had died, and Aeneas, later called Aretas, had succeeded him as king of the Arabs. Syllaeus was endeavouring by spreading slanders to depose Aretas and usurp the throne, and he was handing out large bribes at court and making lavish promises to Caesar himself. Caesar, moreover, was already annoyed with Aretas for having occupied the throne without first writing to obtain his consent.

295

However, Aretas now sent a letter to Caesar, along with gifts including a golden crown worth many talents, and accused Syllaeus of being a corrupt servant who had murdered Obadas by poison and assumed the royal power even in his lifetime; and he also charged him with debauching the wives of the Arabs and with borrowing money so as to secure the kingship for himself. But Caesar took no notice even of these allegations, and dismissed his emissaries without accepting any of the gifts.

296

297

The situation in Judaea and Arabia continued to deteriorate. A state of anarchy prevailed, and as things grew worse there was no one to take a grip on events. One of the kings was still too unsure of his power to deal effectively with law-breakers, while Herod, who had incurred Caesar's displeasure by his swift reprisal, was forced to endure every assault on his authority. Seeing no end to the troubles that surrounded him, he decided once again to send a deputy to Rome, hoping to obtain a more favourable reception through the good offices of his friends and a direct appeal to Caesar. It was Nicolas of Damascus who set out on this mission.

298

299

Mariamme's Sons Imprisoned

300

To coincide with this crisis Herod's domestic life suffered further strain, and his relations with his sons took a serious turn for the worse. Even before, it had not been difficult to see that Fortune had the direst of human tragedies in store for the royal house, but matters now came to a head, for the following reason.

301   There was a Spartan named Eurycles, a man of some distinction in his own country but of bad character, adept at supporting a luxurious lifestyle by the art of flattery, yet without damage to his reputation. Coming to visit Herod he gave him presents, for which he received a still more generous return, and in the king's company he showed a sureness of touch that earned him a place among Herod's

302 closest friends. He lodged with Antipater but was also able to make the acquaintance of Alexander and, by claiming to enjoy the favour of Archelaus of Cappadocia, he became his regular companion.

303   To suit his purpose he pretended also to have a high regard for Glaphyra, and he busied himself in winning the confidence of everyone unobtrusively, always attentive to their words and actions in order to requite their kindness

304 by incriminating them. In his contacts with them he managed to give each of them the impression that it was for him that he reserved his friendship, while associating with the others merely to serve his interests. And in this way he won the trust of Alexander, who was young and fully persuaded that he could speak of his problems safely to Eurycles, but to no one else.

305   Alexander told him bitterly how his father had turned against him, described his mother's fate, and explained how Antipater had usurped their place of honour and was now all-powerful. It was beyond all bearing, he said, for his father was now so deeply set in hatred that he even

306 refused to speak to them at table and on other social occasions. Such were the terms in which he spoke of his sufferings, as was quite natural. But Eurycles reported his words to Antipater, telling him that he was not acting from self-interest, but out of deference to Antipater for the honour he had shown him, and because of the gravity of the matter. And he warned him to be on his guard against Alexander, who had aired his grievances with feeling and with murder in his words.

307   Antipater interpreted this as a gesture of friendship and

made generous gifts to him on a number of occasions.
Finally he persuaded him to inform Herod of the conver-
308 sation, and Eurycles told Herod of Alexander's grudge
against him, explaining that he had his son's own words
as proof. He convinced the king, and the effect of his
cunning and provocative tale was to fill Herod with an
309 implacable hatred – as he showed at once by rewarding
Eurycles with fifty talents. Taking the money, he next went
to Archelaus, king of Cappadocia, to whom he spoke in
praise of Alexander and claimed to have served him well
310 by reconciling him with his father. And he made money
out of Archelaus, too, and then left before his mischief
was detected. Even in Sparta Eurycles continued in his
wicked ways, and eventually he was banished from his
country for his crimes.

311 The king of the Jews was no longer content, as before,
merely to listen to slanders against Alexander and Aristobulus; he now hated them on his own account, and in the
312 absence of accusations he contrived to throw suspicion on
them by watching their every movement, making enquiries
and lending his ear to anyone who had a charge to bring
against them. He was informed* that Euaratus of Cos
was conspiring with Alexander, and this gave Herod the
greatest possible satisfaction.

313 Charges continued to be fabricated against his sons, as
if there were an open competition to tell of some threat
they had posed to the king's life. The young men now
314 suffered a heavier blow. Herod had two bodyguards,
Iucundus and Tyrannus, who were prized for their
strength and stature. But the king quarrelled with them
and dismissed them, and they took to riding with Alexander and his friends, who gave them gold and other gifts
315 as a tribute to their athleticism. The king at once became
suspicious of them and had them tortured, and after a
long resistance they finally said that Alexander had tried
to persuade them to murder Herod when he was casting
his spear in the chase; they could say that he had fallen
from his horse and been run through by his own spears,
an accident that Alexander told them he had suffered
316 before. They also pointed out where there was gold buried
under the floor of a stable, and convicted the hunt-master

of giving them spears belonging to the king and weapons to Alexander's servants, at the young man's bidding.

317   Next, the commandant of the garrison at Alexandreion was arrested and tortured. He was accused of having promised to admit the young men to the fortress and to hand over to them the money that the king had deposited

318   there. He confessed to none of it, but his son came forward to say that it was true, and produced a note, presumably in Alexander's handwriting, which read as follows:

'When we have accomplished, with God's help, all that

319   we proposed, we shall come to you. Stand by your promise and receive us in the fortress.' After this document was produced Herod no longer doubted that his sons were plotting against him, but Alexander said that the scribe Diophantus had copied his handwriting and that the note was a malicious invention of Antipater's. And it is a fact that Diophantus was reputed to be skilled in forgery, and was later convicted of similar offences against others and put to death.

320   The king also brought the men who had been tortured before the people of Jericho, to have them accuse his sons; and the mob closed in on them and stoned them to death.

321   They were eager to kill Alexander and his brother in the same way, but the king prevented it and restrained the crowd with the help of Ptolemy and Pheroras. However, the youths were held in custody and a watch was kept on them. No one was allowed access to them, everything they did or said was observed – they might indeed have been condemned criminals, to suffer such disgrace and fear.

322   One of them, Aristobulus, was so dejected that he tried to win the sympathy of his aunt and mother-in-law, and to turn them against the author of their misfortunes. 'Are you too not in danger of death,' he said to Salome, 'when you stand accused of betraying all the secrets of the palace

323   to Syllaeus, in the hope of marrying him?' Salome was very quick to report these words to her brother, and his patience finally snapped. Ordering them to be put in chains and separately confined, he demanded written confessions, listing all the wrongs they had done their father,

324   to be passed on to Caesar. But when confronted with this demand they wrote that they had neither conceived nor

organised any conspiracy against their father, but had intended to run away; and that they had had no choice in this as their lives had been ruined by the atmosphere of suspicion.

325 About this time there arrived from Cappadocia an emissary of Archelaus, named Melas, who was one of the princes of that king. Herod, wishing to demonstrate Archelaus's ill-will towards him, summoned Alexander in his chains and questioned him further about their intended flight, asking for their destination and how they had planned to travel. Alexander replied that they were to go 326 to Archelaus, who had agreed to have them taken on to Rome; but he denied that they had formed any unnatural or hurtful design against their father, and said that there was no truth in the slanders concocted by the malice of 327 their enemies. He only wished that Tyrannus and his friends were still alive, so that a more reliable interrogation might be held, but Antipater had infiltrated the crowd with his own friends and had them killed too soon.

328 When he said this, Herod gave orders that Melas and Alexander should be taken to Glaphyra, the daughter of Archelaus, and that she should be questioned to establish whether she knew any evidence of a plot against him. 329 When they came to her and Glaphyra saw Alexander in chains, she at once beat her head and cried aloud, in an outburst of grief that touched the heart. The young man also wept, and the others were so distressed at the sight 330 that it was a long time before they felt able to carry out their orders. In the end, Ptolemy, who had been charged with bringing Alexander to his wife, ordered him to state whether she had been aware of his actions, and he replied, 'Of course she was aware of them – I love her more than 331 my own life and she is the mother of my children.' At this Glaphyra protested that she knew of no mischief, but if she could help to save him by falsely accusing herself she would admit everything. But Alexander said, 'No act of impiety, such as they suspect without a shred of justification, was ever entertained by me, nor do you know of any. You know only that we were resolved on making our way to Archelaus, and from there to Rome.'

332 When she acknowledged this, Herod took it as proved

that Archelaus meant him no good. He gave a letter to
Olympus and Volumnius, ordering them to put in at
Elaeusa in Cilicia on their voyage, make Archelaus
acquainted with these developments and reproach him for
333 having a hand in his sons' conspiracy, and then to sail on
to Rome. He further instructed them that, if they found
that Nicolas had had some success in restoring him to
Caesar's favour, they should give him the letter and the
evidence against his sons which he had put together and
334 sent with them. Archelaus said in his defence that he had
agreed to receive the young men out of regard for their
interests and for their father's – he had been anxious to
prevent Herod taking sterner retribution for the defiance
with which they met his suspicions. But he had not, he
said, promised to send them to Caesar, nor made any
other agreement with his sons out of ill-will towards
Herod.

Nicolas Reconciles Augustus with Herod

335 When Herod's representatives landed at Rome, they took
the opportunity to deliver the letter to Caesar, finding him
reconciled with Herod as a result of Nicolas's mission.
336 This had progressed as follows. On arriving in Rome and
presenting himself at court, Nicolas made an initial
decision not only to pursue the particular object of his
337 visit, but also to accuse Syllaeus, for it was obvious that
they had been quarrelling before he appeared. The Arabs,
who deserted Syllaeus and went over to Nicolas, gave him
information about all Syllaeus's crimes, and supplied him
with clear proofs that all Obadas's friends had been
destroyed. At the time of their rupture with Syllaeus they
had held on to letters of his which they now produced to
338 convict him. Nicolas realised that he had had a stroke of
good luck, and used it to further his remaining purpose of
reconciling Caesar with Herod. He was well aware that he
would not obtain an audience to offer a defence of Herod's
conduct, but that if he agreed to prosecute Syllaeus he
would have a chance to say something on Herod's behalf.
339   A day was fixed for the two sides to put their case and,
with Aretas's ambassadors in attendance, Nicolas made a

series of accusations against Syllaeus. He charged him with the murder of the king and many other Arabs, with
340 borrowing money for unlawful purposes, and with committing adultery not only with women in Arabia but also in Rome. He then went on to make his most important charge, that he had deceived Caesar by telling him nothing but lies about Herod's conduct.

341 When he reached this point, Caesar stopped him and said that where Herod was concerned he wanted an answer to one question only: had he led an army into Arabia, killed two and a half thousand of its people, taken prisoners and pillaged the country? Nicolas replied that he
342 could assure him that there was little or no truth in these claims, in the version that Caesar had heard, and that they gave him no good reason to be angry.

343 This was unexpected, and as Caesar listened intently Nicolas referred to the loan of five hundred talents and to the contract, which included a clause empowering Herod to recover his debt from any part of Syllaeus's territory once the agreed time had expired. The campaign, he argued, was not really a campaign at all, but a legitimate
344 means of recovering his own money. Nor had he even acted as promptly as the contract allowed, but had made many approaches to the governors of Syria, Saturninus and Volumnius. Finally, in their presence at Berytus* Syllaeus had sworn a solemn oath by the Fortune of Caesar that within thirty days he would hand over the money and the refugees from Herod's kingdom. But Syl-
345 laeus defaulted, and Herod went again to the governors, who gave him permission to recover the debt. Yet even so, he said, it was with reluctance that Herod took his men beyond his borders.

346 This, then [he went on], was the 'war' – to use their dramatic terminology, and this the nature of the campaign. And yet how could it be a war, when your own governors gave their permission, when the contract provided for it, and when your name, Caesar, and the names of the other gods had been profaned?

347 I must now speak of the prisoners. There were bandits among the people of Trachonitis, forty at first but later

more, who to escape punishment at Herod's hands made
Arabia their base. Syllaeus made them welcome, and supported them to be a threat to the human race. He gave them
348   land to settle on, and shared the profits of their banditry.
But he had agreed under the same oaths to surrender them
within the period fixed for the repayment of the loan, and
to this day he can point to not a single captive, apart from
them, who has been taken from Arab soil. Even of the
bandits not all have been captured, but only those who
349   failed to hide. I submit, therefore, that the charge concerning the prisoners has been exposed as a malicious calumny.

   And now, Caesar, I would have you learn of Syllaeus's
biggest lie, fabricated to arouse your anger. I can assure you
350   that it was only when the Arabs attacked us, and one or
two of Herod's men fell, that he fought to defend himself,
and then with difficulty; and the outcome was that Nakebos
their commander and about twenty-five of them in all were
killed. When Syllaeus alleged that two and a half thousand
lost their lives, he was multiplying each one of them by a
hundred!

351   These words raised Caesar's temper further, and full of
anger he turned to Syllaeus and asked him how many of
the Arabs had been killed. Syllaeus in some confusion said
that he had been deceived, but then the contract relating
to the loan was read, together with letters from the
governors and from all the cities that had complaints to
352   make about the activities of the bandits; and Caesar finally
had a change of heart and condemned Syllaeus to death
while becoming reconciled with Herod. He regretted the
sharp tone of the letter he had sent Herod when influenced
by slander, and said as much to Syllaeus, telling him that
by his lies he had made him act unfairly towards a man
353   who was his friend. The conclusion was that Syllaeus was
sent back to make retribution and repay his creditors, and
after that to suffer punishment.

   With Aretas, however, Caesar was still displeased,
because he had seized power on his own account and
without reference to Caesar. He had decided, in fact, to
give Arabia to Herod, but was dissuaded by Herod's own
354   letter to him; for Olympus and Volumnius, on learning of

the favourable change in Caesar's attitude, had promptly
decided to carry out Herod's instructions and deliver the
355   letter and the evidence concerning his sons. When Caesar
read it he thought that to add another kingdom to Herod's
dominions, when he was old and at variance with his sons,
would be bad policy. Instead, he received the embassy
from Aretas, reproaching him only for his haste in not
waiting for Caesar to confer the royal title, and accepted
his gifts and confirmed him in power.

Mariamme's Sons Tried and Sentenced

356   Following his reconciliation with Herod, Caesar wrote to
him to say that he was distressed by the problem of his
sons and that, if they were guilty of an unnatural crime,
he should use the power permitted to him and punish
them as parricides. On the other hand, if they had planned
357   to run away, he should merely admonish them and spare
their lives. He also advised him to appoint a council and
convene it at Berytus, where there were many Roman
colonists, inviting the Roman governors of Syria, the king
of Cappadocia, Archelaus, and such other close friends
and persons of importance as he thought fit, and to consult
358   their opinion in deciding what action should be taken.
These were Caesar's instructions.

When the letter was delivered to him, Herod was at
once delighted to find Caesar reconciled to him, and
359   delighted too that he had a free hand to act against his
sons. His attitude was already hardened, but the difficulties he had been in had in a way saved him from such a
bold and reckless step as the destruction of his sons. But
now he seized on the improvement in his fortunes and his
new freedom of action to pursue his hatred by an unpre-
360   cedented exercise of power. He sent out invitations, therefore, to all the men he chose to attend his council, but not
to Archelaus. He thought it best not to have him there, as
he was on bad terms with him and perhaps believed that
he would interfere with his plans.

361   The governors and the others whom he invited from the
different cities assembled at Berytus. Herod thought that it
would be unwise to present his sons before the council,

and instead kept them in a Sidonian village called Platana, near the city of Berytus, so that he could produce them if
362 they were summoned. Alone and unaccompanied he appeared before the court, which numbered a hundred and fifty men, and delivered his accusation with none of the anguish he might have felt if driven by ill fortune, and none of the sentiments a father should express towards his sons.

363   His manner, as he sought to establish their guilt, was violent and agitated, vividly reflecting the savage rage that possessed him. He allowed his audience no opportunity to examine the evidence, but supported his case with a tirade against his sons that came disgracefully from the lips of their father. The letters they had written, which he read out, contained no mention of a plot or any thought of filial impiety, but spoke only of their plan to abscond, together with some abusive references to Herod, reproaching him for the grudge he bore them.

364   When he came to these remarks, he raised his voice and magnified the advantage they gave him into a confession that they had formed a plot, swearing that he would sooner lose his life than hear such words. In conclusion,
365 he said that while he personally had the authority to act both by natural right and by the gift of Caesar, it was also a law of their country that, when a man's parents accused him and placed their hands on his head, those present
366 were obliged to stone him to death.* He was ready to do this, he said, in his own country and kingdom, but would await their judgement nevertheless. But they had come there, he suggested, not so much to pass judgement on the manifest wickedness of his sons, which had come close to destroying him, as to take the opportunity of sharing his anger. No one, however far removed, could be justified in disregarding such a conspiracy.

367   After the king made his speech, without admitting the young men even to let them defend themselves, the members of the council agreed together that they had no power to moderate his feelings or effect a reconciliation, and so they confirmed Herod's authority. The first to speak was
368 Saturninus, who as a former consul was a man of considerable influence. Because of the circumstances he took a very

lenient view, saying that although he condemned Herod's sons he did not think it right to put them to death, as he had sons himself and the punishment was too severe even if they were responsible for all Herod's misfortunes.

369   After Saturninus his three sons, who accompanied him as legates, voiced the same opinion, but Volumnius took the opposite view and said that sons guilty of such impious treachery towards their father should be punished by death. Most of the speakers who followed took the same line, so that there now seemed only one verdict: the young men were condemned to death.

Popular Opposition

370 From there Herod at once took them to Tyre, where Nicolas sailed from Rome to meet him. Herod told him what had happened at Berytus, and asked him what his
371 friends in Rome thought about his sons. Nicolas replied that they thought them guilty of impiety in their intentions towards their father, but that he ought to imprison them
372 and hold them in chains. And he went on, 'If you decide on a different punishment, take care not to appear influenced by anger rather than sound judgement. On the other hand, if you decide to release them, make sure that this unhappy problem is resolved. Most of your friends in Rome take the same view.' Herod pondered his advice carefully in silence and then ordered him to sail with him.

373   When he came to Caesarea, everyone at once began to talk of his sons, and the kingdom was in suspense as
374 people waited to see what would become of them. They began to feel a dreadful apprehension that the long feud was reaching its climax; but while they were indignant at the plight of the youths, there was danger in a hasty word, and they bottled up their sympathy, suffering in silence.

375   There was one of them, however, an old soldier named Tiro, whose son was a friend and contemporary of Alexander's, who gave frank expression to all those secret thoughts that others kept to themselves. There were many occasions when he felt compelled to harangue the crowds
376 and speak his mind without reserve. 'Truth,' he would cry, 'is dead, and Justice abolished among men. Lies and

wickedness hold sway, and cast so dark a cloud over things that transgressors are blind even to the worst of human sufferings.'

377 People realised that he was courting danger by such outspokenness, but they were impressed by his good sense
378 and his robust response to the crisis. Everyone was pleased to hear his own thoughts put into words by Tiro, and while they looked after their own safety by keeping quiet they still welcomed his unguarded outbursts. They were expecting a tragedy, and this caused everyone to speak of him.

379 Tiro now, with a total lack of inhibition, pushed his way into the king's presence and requested a private audience. And when Herod agreed, he said, 'Your Majesty, I cannot remain silent when a great tragedy threatens. I have decided to speak out boldly rather than look to my own safety, and you need to hear what I have to say. Indeed you can profit by it if you will put it to good use.

380 'Have you taken leave of your senses? Where is that extraordinary mind that brought all your great ambitions to fulfilment? And why are you destitute of friends and
381 relatives? Not that I count them as friends or relatives, even were they here, when they can look with unconcern on this defilement of a once blessed kingdom!

382 'Will you not consider what is being done? These two young men are the sons of your queen, and accomplished in every virtue: and will you put them to death, and abandon yourself in old age to the care of a son who has
383 ill requited the hope you placed in him, and of relatives whose death sentences you have so often pronounced? Will you not realise that despite their silence the mass of the people can see your guilt and detest your cruelty, and that the whole army with its officers feels pity for the sufferers, and hatred for those responsible?'

384 At the start of this the king listened in a reasonably good humour, but it need scarcely be said that when Tiro referred explicitly to his domestic tragedy and distrust of
385 his relatives he was taken aback. But, with the uninhibited bluntness of a soldier, Tiro pressed doggedly on, his lack of education causing him to go much further than was
386 prudent in the circumstances; and Herod, feeling that he

was being denounced rather than advised to his advantage, lost all his composure. And so he enquired who the disgruntled soldiers and their fractious officers were, and gave orders that all whose names he was given, and Tiro himself, should be put in chains and kept under guard.

387 After this was done, the next person to seize his opportunity was Trypho, one of the king's barbers. This man came forward to say that Tiro had often tried to persuade him to cut the king's throat with his razor, while he was shaving him, and had promised that he would win the

388 special favour of Alexander and be rewarded with expensive gifts. The statement prompted Herod to order his arrest, and Tiro and his son and the barber were subsequently tortured.

389 Tiro could not be broken, but his son could see to what extremity he was reduced, with no hope of survival, and realised from the pain he suffered what was going to happen to himself; and so he told the king that he would let him know the truth if his information would secure

390 their release from further torture and abuse. When Herod gave his word to accept these terms, he said that a plan had been agreed whereby Tiro was to attack and murder the king, who was within easy reach when they were alone together, and if he paid the likely penalty for his deed, it would be a noble fate by virtue of the service he had rendered Alexander.

391 By making this statement he brought an end to his father's torment, but whether he had been forced into telling the truth, or merely said this because he thought it would help him and his father to escape their predicament, is not certain.

The Execution of Alexander and Aristobulus

392 Even if Herod had been in two minds before about killing his own children, he now left no room in his heart for such doubts. Dismissing any consideration that might lead him to change his mind and exercise better judgement, he now made haste to bring his purpose to its conclusion.

393 Calling an assembly, he brought before them the three hundred officers who had been accused, together with Tiro

and his son and the barber who had denounced them, and
394   brought charges against all of them. And the crowd bat-
tered them with whatever came to hand and put them to
death. Alexander and Aristobulus were taken to Sebaste
on their father's order, and executed by strangling.* During the night their bodies were laid at Alexandreion, where
their maternal grandfather and most of their ancestors
were buried.

395   To some it may not appear strange that a long-nurtured
hatred should develop such proportions as to vanquish
the impulses of nature. But one might well pause before
deciding where the blame should be laid. Are we to blame
the young men, who provoked their father's anger to the
limit, and by their persistent defiance made an implacable
396   enemy of him? Or was Herod himself at fault, through his
unfeeling and obsessive desire for power, and glory in all
its forms, and his belief that he must stop at nothing to
get unchallenged possession of everything he wanted?

397   Or again, what part was played by Fortune, who has
power greater than the most prudent calculation, and by
whom, so we are persuaded, the actions of men are
predetermined to an inevitable outcome? We also call her
Fate, as the cause of everything that happens. But as to
398   this doctrine, I believe that no more is needed than to
compare it with the alternative view that attributes some
responsibility to ourselves, and holds us accountable for
the differences in the conduct of our lives – a doctrine
advanced before our time in the Law.*

399   What of my other two proposals? On the one hand,
there are grounds for blaming Herod's sons, who with the
presumption of youth and the self-conceit of royalty were
ready to hear slanders against their father. Uncharitable
critics of his life and career, they were suspicious to the
point of malice and unbridled in their speech; and on both
accounts they fell easy prey to those who watched them
and denounced them for their own ends.

400   Their father, on the other hand, must forfeit our respect
for that act of impiety against his sons. He had no clear
proof of a conspiracy and failed to convict them of
preparing an attempt on his life, yet he brought himself to
kill his own flesh and blood – handsome young men whom

every nation loved, well versed in the arts of hunting and of warfare, and accomplished speakers on topics of the moment. All these virtues belonged to them, and especially to the elder, Alexander.

401   It would have been enough for Herod, even after condemning them, to keep them alive, either in prison or in exile from his kingdom; he was protected by the power of Rome, a mighty shield that made him invulnerable to
402   violent assault. But to kill them in such haste and to gratify the passion that mastered him showed a lack of religious scruple that defies assessment. How could a man of his age commit so grave a crime?*

403   Nor is the fact that he delayed and temporised a reason to excuse him. For a man suddenly distraught or under provocation to act irrationally is a common occurrence, serious though it may be. But to deliberate at length, with many starts and many hesitations, and then at last to take it on and see it through: this was the act of a murderous
404   mind that nothing could divert from evil. He showed this also later on when he spared not even his closest friends among those who survived. Their deaths may have aroused less sympathy because of the justice of their punishment, but his cruelty was just as evident in refusing mercy even to them. We shall deal fully with this in the following pages.

BOOK XVII

Antipater Plots Against Herod

1 Antipater had disposed of his brothers, and implicated his father in the most heinous of crimes that cried to heaven for vengeance. But his hopes for his own future were not at all what he had intended. He had no need to fear that he might have to share power with his brothers, yet he found the path to the throne more difficult and inaccessible for him because of the great hatred that the people had

2 come to feel for him. This was indeed a problem, but he was still more worried by the hostile attitude of the army, on whom the whole security of the royal house depended at times of national unrest. So great was the danger he had courted by destroying his brothers.

3 Even so, it remained true that he shared power with his father and was king in all but name, and he enjoyed Herod's confidence and goodwill all the more by claiming – and he deserved to perish for it – that he had denounced his brothers to protect Herod's life, and not out of enmity towards them and, before that, towards their father. Such was the accursed madness that assailed him.

4 All this, of course, served Antipater as a means of attacking Herod, by getting rid of people who might denounce him for what he was planning to do, and by ensuring that Herod would have no support to fall back

5 on when Antipater emerged openly as his enemy. It was out of hatred for his father that he carried out the plot against his brothers, and he pursued his purpose all the more tenaciously because he realised that, whereas the throne would certainly be his if Herod died, he would be in deep danger if the king's life were prolonged: the crime he had planned would be revealed, and his father would be forced to become his enemy. Accordingly he spared no

6   expense in courting the favour of his father's friends, using large bribes to overcome people's dislike of him; and he took particular pains to ingratiate himself with Herod's friends at Rome by sending them expensive presents, and

7   above all with Saturninus, the legate of Syria. He also hoped to win over Saturninus's brother by lavishing gifts on him, and used the same technique with the king's sister, who was married to one of Herod's closest confidants.

He proved to be an extremely clever person at feigning friendship and gaining the trust of the company he kept,

8   and most accomplished also at concealing his hatreds. His aunt, however, was not fooled – she had seen through him long before and was immune to his deceit, having taken

9   every precaution to resist his malice. Even so, her daughter, a girl formerly married to Aristobulus, became the wife of Antipater's maternal uncle,* and it was Antipater who conceived and arranged the match. Salome's other daughter was married to the son of her husband Calleas.* But the marriage alliance did nothing to hinder her perception of his evil character, any more than the earlier relationship had altered her hatred of Aristobulus.

10   Salome herself had set her heart on marrying Syllaeus the Arab, with whom she was in love, but Herod forced her to marry Alexas, and he had an ally in Julia, who persuaded Salome that to reject the match would bring her into open conflict with Herod, who had sworn that his goodwill towards her would be conditional on her agreeing to marry Alexas. And so Salome let Julia persuade her, both because she was Caesar's wife and because her advice generally turned out for the best. Meanwhile Herod sent

11   back Alexander's wife* to her father, King Archelaus, and returned the dowry out of his private funds, to prevent any dispute arising between them.

12   Herod personally brought up his sons' children, and did so most conscientiously. Alexander had had two boys by Glaphyra* and Aristobulus three boys and two girls* by

13   Berenice, the daughter of Salome. Once, in the company of friends, he presented the young children and, after lamenting the fate of his sons, prayed that nothing like it would befall their children, and that by growing in virtue and the practice of righteousness they would repay him

14 for their upbringing. He also arranged marriages for them in anticipation of their coming of age. Alexander's elder son was betrothed to the daughter of Pheroras, and Aristobulus's eldest son to the daughter of Antipater;* the two daughters of Aristobulus were engaged to Antipater's son and to his own son Herod.* This Herod had been born to the king by the daughter of the high priest, for the king had several wives at the same time, as is traditional among us.

15   He arranged these betrothals for the. children because he pitied them as orphans and because he hoped that the marriage alliance would induce Antipater to feel kindly disposed to them.

16 Antipater, however, adopted the same policy towards his brothers' sons as to their fathers, and his father's patronage of them vexed him. He could foresee them becoming more powerful than his brothers, especially when they reached manhood; for as grandsons of Archelaus, they would have a king as their ally, while Pheroras, who was a tetrarch, would give his support to

17 his daughter's future husband. He was also alert to the feelings of the people as a whole, who pitied the orphans and hated him for the extreme lengths to which he had taken his malice towards his brothers. And so he contrived to get his father's arrangements dissolved, seeing the danger to himself if they were destined to acquire such power.

18 Herod yielded to his request and by a change of plan betrothed Aristobulus's daughter to Antipater and Pheroras's daughter to his son; and so the marriage arrangements were altered against the wishes of the king.

19   King Herod at this time had nine wives. These included the mother* of Antipater, and the daughter of the high priest, who bore him his son Herod; a daughter of his

20 brother and also a cousin,* both of whom were childless; and a Samaritan woman,* who had two sons, Antipas and Archelaus, and a daughter Olympias. Joseph, the king's nephew,* later married Olympias, while Archelaus and Antipas were brought up in Rome by a Jew. His other

21 wives were Cleopatra, a woman of Jerusalem, who bore him two sons, Herod and Philip, who was also brought up in Rome; Pallas, by whom he had a son called Phasael;

22 Phaedra; and Elpis, the mother of his two daughters

Roxane and Salome. His eldest daughters,* whose mother
was Mariamme, the mother of Alexander and Aristobulus,
and whom Pheroras had refused to marry, he gave in
marriage to Antipater, his sister's son, and to Phasael, the
son of his brother Phasael. This, then, was Herod's family.

Babylonian Jews Settled in Batanaea

23 At this time he needed to secure himself against attack by
the Trachonites, and decided to build a village the size of
a city between them and the Jews, to protect his own land
from invasion and to serve as a forward base from which
he could mount surprise attacks and damage his enemy.
24 He learned that a Jew from Babylonia had crossed the
Euphrates with five hundred mounted archers and about a
hundred of his kinsmen, and that he happened to be
residing in Syria, at Daphne in Antioch. Saturninus, who
25 was then governor of Syria, had given him a place named
Ulatha to settle in. Herod sent for this man with his troop
of followers and promised to provide him with land in the
toparchy called Batanaea, which bordered on Trachonitis,
intending to make his settlement into a buffer zone; and
he declared the territory exempt from taxes and all the
customary forms of tribute, offering them the land to
make their home in without obligation.
26   Attracted by these terms, the Babylonian went and took
possession of the land, where he built fortresses and a
village which he called Bathyra. He now offered protection
against Trachonite banditry both to the local people adjacent to Trachonitis and to Jews from Babylonia who came
to sacrifice in Jerusalem; and many people of Jewish faith
27 came from all parts to join him. His land became heavily
populated because of its complete exemption from taxation, a concession which its people enjoyed throughout
Herod's lifetime. Herod's successor, his son Philip,*
28 imposed light taxes on them for a brief period, but then
Agrippa the Great and his son of the same name* made
quite exorbitant demands on them, while still allowing
them their freedom. Power has now passed to the Romans,
who continue to respect their free status but have subjected

them to a crushing burden of tribute. I shall deal with
these matters in more detail in the course of my narrative.

29   Zamaris, the Babylonian recruited by Herod to occupy
this land, died. He had lived a good life, and left worthy
sons to follow him, and none more so than Jacimus,* a
man of outstanding valour who organised his Babylonian
followers into a company of cavalry. It was a troop of

30 these men who served the kings as bodyguards. When
Jacimus died in old age he left a son named Philip, an
expert at physical combat who could bear comparison
with any man for his other qualities besides. In conse-

31 quence, a firm bond of friendship and lasting goodwill was
formed between him and King Agrippa, and he regularly
trained whatever army the king maintained and led it on
its campaigns.

Pheroras in Disgrace

32 With Herod distracted as I have described, the entire
responsibility of government rested on Antipater. He was
not averse to using his authority to enforce his own wishes,
as his father felt assured of his loyalty and trust and was
happy to defer to him; and he was emboldened to extend
his authority over others by his father's ignorance of his

33 sinister purpose and total confidence in his word. He was
a formidable opponent to them all, not so much because
of the power his authority gave him as because of the
foresight with which his malice pursued its victims.

   Pheroras especially paid court to him, and was courted
in return. Antipater had used great cunning to get him
ensnared by enlisting the women of the house to deal with

34 him, since Pheroras had become enslaved to his wife, and
to her mother and sister, even though Herod hated them
for their insulting treatment of his maiden daughters.* In
spite of all, Pheroras endured his lot and could do nothing
without the women; they held the wretched man under
their spell and had a friendly agreement among themselves

35 to act in concert on all occasions. Antipater therefore had
them completely in his power, both through his own
influence and his mother's, since the four of them spoke
with one voice.

Differences of opinion that arose between Pheroras and
Antipater were concerned with matters of no real impor-
36 tance, but they met opposition from the king's sister, who
had been observing everything closely for a long time and,
realising that the purpose of their alliance was to damage
37 Herod, had no inhibitions about informing against them.
For their part, they recognised that their friendship would
be unwelcome to the king, and hit on the idea of keeping
their meetings secret and pretending to hate and abuse
each other when an occasion presented itself, and particularly in the presence of Herod or anyone likely to report
their behaviour. Privately, meanwhile, they worked to
strengthen their alliance.

38 But none of their machinations escaped Salome, either
when they first formed their plan or when they were ready
to act on it. She found out everything and revealed it to
her brother with lurid exaggeration, telling him of secret
meetings and drinking parties and of planning sessions
arranged in private. All this concealment, she said, could
39 have only one meaning – it was a plot to destroy him.
Overtly they might be quarrelsome, with not a good word
to exchange, but they were doing this to keep their friendship from public knowledge, and when they were alone
together they were on good terms and united in their
hostility towards those whom they were at such pains to
keep in ignorance of their pact. But although Salome
40 would go to her brother and give him details of her
findings, most of which he was already aware of on his
own account, he lacked the confidence to act out of
suspicion of his sister's charges.

41 There was also a Jewish sect, known as Pharisees, proud
of their scrupulous observance of ancestral custom and
professing obedience to the laws beloved of God, who had
a powerful hold over the women of the palace; and though
by their foresight they had the power to be of great service
to the king, they were openly resolved on attacking and
42 damaging him. When, for example, the entire Jewish
nation took an oath of loyalty to Caesar and to the king's
government, these men, who were over six thousand in
number, refused to swear the oath; and when the king
punished them with a fine, Pheroras's wife paid the fine

for them. Now they were believed to be inspired by God
with knowledge of the future, and they requited her
43 friendly gesture by foretelling that God had decreed an
end to the power of Herod and his descendants, and that
the royal title would devolve upon her and Pheroras and
their children.

44 Salome got to know of this and reported it to the king,
and further alleged that the Pharisees had corrupted some
of his courtiers. The king thereupon put to death the
principal culprits among the Pharisees, along with Bagoas,
his eunuch, and one Karos, a young man of unrivalled
beauty who was the king's lover. He also killed everyone
in his household who approved of the Pharisees' pro-
45 nouncement. Bagoas had been excited by their promise
that he would be called father and benefactor by command
of one who would be appointed king, and who would be
all-powerful and enable Bagoas to marry and father children of his own.

46 After Herod had punished the Pharisees convicted on
these counts, he held a council of his friends and made
accusations against Pheroras's wife, blaming the woman's
effrontery for the insults suffered by the maidens and
charging her with showing disrespect to himself by such
47 conduct. It was she, he concluded, who had set him at
odds with his brother and who had said and done everything in her power to stir up an unnatural war between
them. And the fine he had imposed on the Pharisees had
been evaded, he said, in consequence of her payments, and
she had a hand nowadays in everything that was done.

48 'In view of this, Pheroras,' he went on, 'it would be
better if you were to get rid of this woman, not at my
request or out of deference to my judgement, but of your
own accord, for she will be the cause of war between us.
If you claim to be my kinsman, give up your wife now –
and you will continue to be my brother and not betray
your love for me.'

49 Pheroras, though disconcerted by the force of these
words, replied that it would not be right to give up either
his relationship with his brother or his devotion to his
wife, and that he would rather die than face life without
50 the woman he loved. Herod was angered by his attitude

and would gladly have punished Pheroras for it, but he restrained himself. He did, however, forbid Antipater and his mother to associate with Pheroras, and ordered them
51 to prevent the women meeting together. And they agreed to this; but Pheroras and Antipater continued to meet and make merry together at every opportunity. Word even got about that Pheroras's wife was intimate with Antipater and that Antipater's mother was helping to promote the liaison.

Antipater sent to Rome

52 Feeling distrustful of his father and afraid that his hatred of him might grow stronger, Antipater wrote to his friends in Rome, telling them to instruct Herod to send Antipater
53 to Caesar with all speed. This was done, and Herod sent Antipater on his way, giving him some exceptionally fine presents to take with him, and also a will in which he nominated Antipater as his successor with the provision that, if Antipater predeceased him, then his son Herod, whose mother was the high priest's daughter, would become king.

54 Syllaeus the Arab, who had carried out none of Caesar's commands, set sail at the same time as Antipater, and Antipater repeated before Caesar the charges that Nicolas had brought previously. Syllaeus was further accused by Aretas of having killed many men of note in Petra, in defiance of his own wishes, including Soaemus, a most honourable man of the highest integrity, and of having murdered Fabatus, a slave of Caesar's.

55 And these were not the only charges that he faced. Herod had a bodyguard named Corinthus, who enjoyed the king's complete confidence. Syllaeus offered him a large bribe to kill Herod, and he accepted, but when Fabatus heard of this from Syllaeus's own mouth he
56 reported it to the king. Herod then arrested and tortured Corinthus and the whole plot was revealed to him. He also arrested two other Arabs on the evidence supplied by Corinthus, one a sheikh, the other a friend of Syllaeus;
57 and these also confessed under torture that they had come to strengthen Corinthus's resolve and to lend a hand in

the murder if they were needed. Herod acquainted Saturninus with all of this, and he sent them off to Rome.

Antipater Accused

58 Pheroras remained steadfast in his devotion to his wife,
and when Herod ordered him to retire to his own tetrarchy
he was glad to leave, and swore a solemn oath never to
return until he heard that Herod was dead. Even when the
king fell ill and he was asked to go back to receive
confidential instructions, in case the king should die, he
honoured his oath by refusing the request. Pheroras had
59 declared his intention in advance, yet he was not followed
in this by Herod, who came unsolicited to his brother
when he later became ill himself. And when Pheroras died
Herod had his body prepared and brought to Jerusalem,
where he gave him an honourable burial and decreed a
period of solemn mourning for him.

60   This was the start of Antipater's downfall, though at
the time he had sailed to Rome. God was punishing him
for the murder of his brothers, and I shall give a full
account of it to serve as an example and a warning to
mankind to live righteously in all circumstances.

61   After the death and burial of Pheroras, two worthy
freedmen of his came to Herod and begged him not to
leave his dead brother unavenged but to investigate the
unexplained and unfortunate manner of his passing. They
62 seemed trustworthy, and, when Herod showed interest in
what they had to say, they told him that Pheroras, who
had dined with his wife on the day before he became ill,
had been served an unusual concoction containing a drug,
and had died from eating it. The drug, they added, had
been brought by a woman from Arabia, and though it had
been described as a love-potion, designed for sexual
arousal, its real purpose was to kill Pheroras.

63   The women of Arabia are experts in the use of drugs,
and it was admitted that the woman charged with this was
a close friend of Syllaeus's mistress, and that Pheroras's
mother-in-law and sister-in-law had gone to her together
to persuade her to sell the drug, and had brought her back
with them on the day before the meal.

64   The king was incensed at these disclosures and pro-
      ceeded to torture the women's slaves and some of their
      freedwomen. None of them would speak out, and the
      truth remained hidden, until finally one of the women
      surrendered to her pain and called upon God to inflict the
      same torments on Antipater's mother, as the cause of their
      suffering.

65   She said no more, but it gave Herod his clue, and by
      torturing the women he uncovered the whole plot. They
      told him of the carousing and secret meetings, and how
      remarks made privately by Herod to his son had been
      passed on to the women of Pheroras's household – how
      he had ordered Antipater, for example, to keep quiet about
      a gift of a hundred talents he had given him on condition
66   that he broke off all intercourse with Pheroras. They also
      said that Antipater hated his father, and used to complain
      to his mother that his father was dragging out his life to
      the bitter end, and that he was staring old age in the face
      himself and would never have the same enjoyment of the
      royal power even if it came to him. He had also said, they
      alleged, that there were many of his brothers and their
      sons besides who were being trained for kingship, making
      his own hopes altogether insecure, and that he was sure
67   that even now, if anything happened to him, Herod would
      name his brother rather than his son as his successor. And
      he accused the king of barbarous cruelty and the murder
      of his sons, and he and Pheroras, out of fear that Herod
      would attack them too, had already planned their escape,
      Antipater leaving for Rome and Pheroras for his own
      tetrarchy.

68   These statements, which corroborated the allegations
      made by Herod's sister, dispelled any doubts he still felt
      about their reliability. The king was convinced that Anti-
      pater's mother Doris was implicated in his crimes, and
      after confiscating all her finery, worth many talents, he
      dismissed her from the palace. He also made his peace
      with the women belonging to Pheroras.

69   But it was a steward of Antipater, a Samaritan also
      called Antipater, who did most to provoke the king's anger
      against his son. Under torture one of the statements he
      made was that Antipater had had a deadly drug prepared

and had given it to Pheroras with the instruction to give it
to his father while Antipater was abroad, so providing him
70 with the perfect alibi. The drug had been brought from
Egypt by Antiphilus, one of Antipater's friends, and conveyed to Pheroras by Theudion, the maternal uncle of the
king's son Antipater. Pheroras had then given the drug to
the safe keeping of his wife.

71   The king questioned her about this and she confessed it;
and then, running off as if to fetch the drug, she flung
herself down from the roof, though she was saved from
72 death by landing on her feet. Herod revived her and
promised immunity to her and her household on condition
that she made no attempt to hide the truth, but threatened
to break her by the most exquisite tortures if she set herself
to defy him. She gave her word and took an oath that she
would tell the whole story just as it happened – indeed, it
was generally agreed that she told the truth about
everything.

73   'The drug,' she said, 'was brought from Egypt by Antiphilus, who had been supplied with it by his brother, a
physician. Theudion brought it to us, and Pheroras gave it
to me for safe keeping. Antipater had had it prepared to
be used against you.

74   'Now, when Pheroras fell ill and you came and looked
after him, he could see the concern you felt for him and
was heartbroken. He called for me and said, "Wife, Antipater has hoodwinked me. He planned the death of his
father – my own brother – and supplied the drug for the
purpose, but my brother, I can see now, is as good to me
75 as ever. I cannot hope to live much longer, and I would
not wish to go to my forefathers with fratricide in my
heart. Go and fetch the drug, and burn it before my
eyes."' And she brought it and made no delay in carrying
76 out her husband's orders. In fact, although she burned
most of the drug she saved just a little, so that, if the king
should treat her badly after Pheroras died, she could use it
to take her life and escape her torments.

77   This was the account she gave, and she then produced
the drug and the box. Another brother of Antiphilus and
his mother were tortured and in their agony confirmed her
78 account and identified the box. Also accused was the high

priest's daughter, the king's wife, who was said to have known of the whole plot and done her best to conceal it. Herod therefore divorced her and struck her son out of his will, in which he was named as his successor;* and he removed his father-in-law Simon, the son of Boethus, from the office of high priest and replaced him with Matthias, the son of Theophilus, a native of Jerusalem.

79 Meanwhile a freedman of Antipater, Bathyllus, arrived from Rome, and was found under torture to have brought a drug to give to Antipater's mother and Pheroras, which
80 they could use to kill the king if the first one proved ineffective. Letters now came to Herod from his friends in Rome, written at the suggestion of the scheming Antipater, which accused Archelaus and Philip of slandering their father with the murder of Aristobulus and Alexander, and of indulging in self-pity over a summons from their father
81 – a summons which they interpreted as nothing less than an invitation to join the dead. His friends obliged Antipater in this matter in return for large bribes.

Antipater also wrote personally to his father about his young sons, declaring that he fully acquitted them of the most serious charges and excusing their words as an indiscretion of youth. He was occupied at the time with his suit against Syllaeus and busy courting men of influence, and he laid out two hundred talents on expensive
82 clothing, furnishing and ornaments. It may seem surprising that he remained unaware of the serious moves that had been made against him in Judaea seven months earlier, but this is explained by the careful watch that was kept on the roads and the popular hatred he inspired. There was no one eager to risk his own life to protect the position of Antipater.

Antipater Tried and Denounced to Augustus

83 Herod received word from Antipater that he would return at once when all his business had been properly concluded. In replying, he disguised his anger and requested him not to delay on his journey in case anything happened to him in Antipater's absence. He also included some small charges against Antipater's mother, but promised to drop

his complaints against her on his arrival, and made every
effort to appear friendly towards him. He was afraid that
84 if Antipater became suspicious he might postpone his
return, and remain instead in Rome, where he could plot
against Herod's throne with some hope of success.

85   Antipater received this letter in Cilicia. The news of
Pheroras's death had already reached him at Tarentum
and he was bitterly disappointed – not out of any affection
for Pheroras but because he had died without carrying out
his promise to kill his father. Arriving at Celenderis in
86 Cilicia, Antipater was now uncertain whether to complete
his homeward voyage, as he deeply resented his mother's
expulsion from the palace. Some of his friends advised him
to stay there and keep a close watch on events, but others
urged him to sail home without delay, arguing that
any charge against him would collapse on his arrival –
as matters stood it was only his absence that gave his
accusers' case any force.

87   This point persuaded him, and he set sail and put in at
the harbour of Sebastos, which Herod had built at great
88 expense and named Sebastos in honour of Caesar. It was
now that Antipater realised his predicament by the evidence of his own eyes. No one came up to him to greet
him and wish him good luck, as they had on his departure,
but quite the opposite. Abandoning discretion, they met
him with curses on their lips in the belief that he was on
his way to pay the penalty for his brothers' deaths.

89   At just that time Quintilius Varus happened to be in
Jerusalem. He had been sent to succeed Saturninus as
governor of Syria,* and at Herod's request had come in
90 person to advise him about the current crisis. It was while
they were talking together that Antipater appeared, quite
unaware of what had been happening, and entered the
palace still wearing his purple robe. The doorkeepers
admitted him, but barred the way to his friends.

91   Realising how far things had gone he was now thoroughly alarmed, and his fears were confirmed when he
went up to his father to embrace him. Herod pushed him
away, accusing him of fratricide and of plotting his father's
death, and told him that Varus would hear and judge the
92 whole case on the following day. No sooner had he

learned of the grave danger that threatened him than the blow was about to fall, and he left in confusion. He was met by his mother and his wife, the daughter of Antigonus, Herod's predecessor as king of the Jews, and learned the whole story from them. And he then prepared himself for his ordeal.

93 The next day Varus and the king sat in council. Those invited to attend were the friends of both sides, the king's relatives including his sister Salome, witnesses who had been tortured and were to give evidence, and finally some slaves of Antipater's mother who had been arrested shortly before his arrival. They had been carrying a letter containing a warning to Antipater that he should not return home, as his father had discovered everything, and that Caesar was the only refuge left to him, as long as he escaped his father's clutches.

94 Antipater now fell on his knees before his father and begged him not to prejudge the issue, insisting that he could clear his name if he were allowed a hearing. But Herod ordered him to be brought before the court, and then spoke bitterly of his regret at having fathered sons who had caused him such unhappiness. He had not yet recovered, he said, from the malice shown him by his former sons, yet found his old age under threat from the scheming of Antipater. He described how he had brought them up and educated them, and had been generous of his

95 wealth to give them everything they ever wanted. But none of this, he declared, had hindered them from plotting against his life. They had aimed to take his throne before their time, in disobedience to the laws of filial piety, rather than receive it with their father's blessing in the course of nature, as justice required.

96 As for Antipater, he continued, he wondered what high ambition he had entertained that he should dare to go to such unscrupulous lengths. He was named in his father's will as his successor to the throne, and even in his father's lifetime enjoyed the same pomp of majesty and exercise of power. He received an annual income of fifty talents, and had been given the sum of three hundred talents for his journey to Rome.

97 Finally, Herod reproached him with the death of his

brothers. If they were guilty of the charges he brought against them, he said, then Antipater had followed their
98 example, while if they were not, his attacks on relatives so close to him had been to no purpose. He himself had learned the whole story from information provided by Antipater, and no one else, and it was on Antipater's advice that he had acted against them; and now, by inheriting their parricide, Antipater was absolving them of any guilt.

99 As he said this he burst into tears and was unable to go on. Nicolas of Damascus, his friend and constant companion, who was familiar with his way of doing things, was then asked by the king to continue his speech, and gave details of the evidence needed to establish a conviction.

100 Antipater now turned to his father to offer his defence. Recalling all the ways in which Herod had favoured him and citing the honours he had received, he argued that they would never have been given him unless he had deserved them by behaving honourably towards his father. Whenever foresight had been needed he had always shown
101 prudence in making his plans, and when action was called for, everything had been accomplished by his own efforts. And was it likely, after rescuing his father from the plots of others, that he would himself plot against him, and destroy the good name he had won previously by the infamy that this would bring on him?

102 What was more, he had been designated as the king's successor, and was already allowed the enjoyment of the honours appropriate to his position. Was it likely, when he had half the royal power at no risk to himself and without stain to his honour, that he would court condemnation and danger by grasping at the whole, with no certainty of success? Had he not witnessed the punishment of his brothers? He had denounced them and accused them when they might have escaped detection, and when their crime against their father was revealed he had been
103 responsible for their punishment. His efforts in that business were proof that he had conducted himself towards his father with unqualified loyalty.

Of his behaviour in Rome he had a witness in Caesar,

who could no more be deceived than God Himself. There
104 was proof of it in a letter sent by Caesar, which ought to
carry no less weight than the slanders of people whose
purpose was to make trouble between them. The case
against him had been largely fabricated during his absence
abroad, which gave his enemies an opportunity they would
105 not have had if he had been at home. He concluded by
dismissing as lies the evidence given under torture, on the
ground that its victims in their agony naturally make most
of their statements to oblige their tormentors. He then
offered himself for torture.

106   On hearing this defence the council had a change of
heart. His tears and distraught expressions aroused deep
sympathy, so that even his enemies pitied him. Even Herod
now appeared to be wavering in his purpose, although
unwilling to show it.

Nicolas then began to speak, repeating the arguments
advanced by the king with rhetorical emphasis on the
gravity of the charges, and summed up the evidence for
107 the prosecution obtained under torture and from witnesses. In particular he dwelt at length on the king's good
nature in bringing up and educating his sons with nothing
to show for it but a continuous succession of troubles.
108 Even so, he said, he was less surprised by the ill-advised
behaviour of Herod's late sons, in disregarding the right-
eous claims of nature and seeking to obtain power before
their time – they had been very young and corrupted by
109 evil counsellors. But Antipater's heinous offence was quite
astounding. His calculating ambition had not been molli-
fied by his father's kindnesses, as if he belonged to a
particularly venomous species of snake – though even
these are soft enough to spare those who look after them.
And even his brothers' fate had not deterred him from
imitating their monstrous crime.

110   Yet it was you yourself, Antipater [he went on], who
denounced your brothers for their audacious plot, you who
conducted the enquiry, and you who punished them when
they were caught. It is not the indignation you felt towards
them or your zeal in pursuing them that we complain of,
but your eager haste to imitate their irresponsible behav-

iour, which quite takes our breath away. Your purpose, we discover, was never to protect your father, but to destroy your brothers, and to be taken for a loving son through your hatred of their wickedness. You would then have greater licence to carry out your own evil design against

111   him, as your subsequent actions have proved. You did away with your brothers by demonstrating their guilt, yet failed to expose their accomplices, leaving no room for doubt that

112   you were in league with them against your father and undertook their prosecution to ensure that you alone would profit from the plot to murder him.

You had set yourself two tasks, and hoped in each case to enjoy a success in keeping with your character. Against your brothers you proceeded openly, and your pride in your

113   triumph would have been justified but for the fact that you were worse than they. Your plot against your father, on the other hand, you conducted in secret, and you hated your brothers not for conspiring against their father – why, in that case, would you have had the presumption to follow their example? – but because they had a better right than

114   you to succeed to his throne. After disposing of your brothers you meant to lose no time in murdering your father – otherwise you would be quickly convicted of bringing false charges against them. Your aim was to make your unhappy father pay the penalty that your own criminal conduct deserved.

And this was no common parricide that you planned, but

115   one without precedent in recorded history. You, as his son, were plotting not only against your father, but against a father who loved you and was your benefactor. You actually shared the royal power and had been designated as his successor. You were permitted to have the enjoyment of that authority in advance, and you had your father's decision in writing to secure your ambitions for the future.

116   But in assessing the situation you were evidently influenced not by Herod's goodness but by your own evil purpose. Your father deferred to you in everything, yet you desired to rob him even of that share of power that he retained, and while professing to protect him you were acting to destroy him.

117   And your personal wickedness was not all. You filled

your mother with your schemes, you turned the goodwill between your brothers into strife, and you dared to describe your father as a brute – you, whose instincts were crueller than any serpent's, and who used the venom of the serpent against your nearest kin and your greatest benefactor! You enlisted the help of guards and the cunning wiles of men and women to defend yourself against your father, as if 118 your own mind were incapable of acting out the hatred it concealed. You have had free men and slaves tortured, and men and women denounced by your accomplices, and today you have come here eager to deny the truth, and fully resolved to banish from the earth not only your own father, but also the Law that condemns you, the probity of Varus 119 and the nature of Justice. Have you such confidence in your own impudence as to ask to be tortured, while branding as lies the evidence already obtained by torture? Are confessions that serve to protect your father to be rejected as false, whereas your word under torture should be trusted?

120		Varus, I appeal to you. Will you not save the king from the abuse of his kinsman? Will you not do away with this evil beast, who feigned loyalty to his father merely to destroy his brothers, and when assured that he would soon occupy the throne himself proved a deadlier menace to the king than anyone? You know that parricide is an offence, both against nature and against humanity, when it is detected no less than when it is planned, and that to fail to punish it is itself an offence against nature.

121		Nicolas then went on to mention other evidence. There were remarks made to certain people by Antipater's mother, with a woman's loquacity; the consulting of oracles and sacrifices directed against the king; Antipater's drunken orgies with the women of Pheroras; and the confessions obtained under torture and the statements of witnesses. These were many and various, some prepared in advance and others thought up on the spot to provide 122 new evidence or to confirm the findings; for there were people who had stayed silent about Antipater's activities for fear of his being acquitted and taking vengeance on them, but now, when they saw that he was vulnerable to the accusations brought by the leading witnesses, they

123 indulged their hatred of him to the full. Those who came forward to lay charges were driven not by enmity but by the shocking audacity of the crimes he had conceived and his malevolence towards his father and brothers: he had filled the house with strife and mutual destruction, his hatred reckless of justice and his friendship motivated not by loyalty but by calculated regard for his own advantage.

124 All of this had long been familiar to most observers, and especially to those whose habit was to judge events dispassionately by an appeal to moral criteria. Previously they had been deterred from raising an outcry, but their new immunity led them to disclose everything they knew. Proof

125 of his crimes came from many kinds of evidence, and there were no grounds on which it might be discredited as lies. The majority of witnesses spoke out neither from loyalty to Herod nor from fear that they risked being accused of withholding information, but only because they considered Antipater's conduct depraved and believed that he deserved the ultimate penalty, not to protect Herod, but

126 for his own depravity. Many statements were made by numerous witnesses who had not been called to testify, and Antipater, though he had always been an expert at lying without a blush, had not even the strength to raise his voice in contradiction.

127 When Nicolas had concluded the case for the prosecution, Varus ordered Antipater to defend himself, if he had any grounds for pleading innocent of the charges made against him; and he expressed the fervent hope – a hope he said he knew that Antipater's father shared for the same reason – that he would be found not guilty of any crime.

128 Antipater, who had collapsed and was lying prone, thereupon called on God and all mankind to bear witness that he had done no wrong, and to furnish clear testimony that he had not plotted against his father.

129 It is the common practice of men deficient in moral virtue, when embarking on a course of crime, to dismiss the idea of God's omnipresence and proceed to act from their own selfish purpose; but when caught and threatened with retribution, they invoke His name to overthrow all

130 the evidence against them. And this was how Antipater

behaved. He had executed all his plans as if God did not exist, but now, trapped in the snares of justice and lacking any other plea with which to refute the charges, he insulted God's righteousness once again by calling as his witness the God whose testimony he had scorned (in accordance with His will) – testimony that revealed his audacious and sustained campaign against his father.

131 After questioning Antipater repeatedly and hearing no more than invocations of God's name, Varus realised that he was getting nowhere and ordered the drug to be produced to find out what potency it still had. It was

132 brought in, and a prisoner condemned to death drank it at Varus's order and died instantly. At this Varus rose and left the council, and the next day departed for Antioch, which as the capital of Syria was his usual place of

133 residence. Herod at once put his son in chains, and though the people were not informed of Varus's interview with him or what he had said on his departure, they guessed that it was on his advice that he had treated Antipater in this way. After imprisoning him, Herod sent a written account of him to Caesar in Rome, and also envoys to tell Caesar of his villainy.

134 During these same days a letter was intercepted, written to Antipater by Antiphilus, who was staying in Egypt. The king opened it, and its contents were as follows. 'I have sent you the letter from Acme without regard to the risk to my own life. As you know, if I am found out I shall

135 again be in danger from two houses. But I wish you good luck in the matter.' These were the contents of the letter.

The king then looked for the other letter but there was no sign of it, and Antiphilus's slave, who was carrying the

136 letter just read, denied that he had been given another. The king, therefore, was at a loss how to proceed, but then one of his friends noticed that the slave – who was wearing two tunics – had a patch sewn on the undergarment and guessed that the letter was hidden in this pocket. This proved to be the case, and they seized the letter,

137 which read as follows. 'Acme to Antipater. I have written to your father the sort of letter you wanted, and made a copy of the letter I wrote to my mistress in Salome's name.

138 When he reads it I am sure that he will punish Salome for

plotting against him.' The letter to Acme's mistress purporting to come from Salome had been written, as regards its meaning, at the suggestion of Antipater, but in Salome's name and composed in her style.

139 ⸱ Acme had written as follows. 'Acme to King Herod. I make it my business to let you know of any threats against you. I have found a letter of Salome's in which she complains of you to my mistress, and I have risked my life to help you by making a copy and sending it to you. Salome wrote it because she wants to marry Syllaeus. Tear this letter up, so that my life too may not be in danger.'

140 Her letter to Antipater had been to inform him that she had followed his instruction and written to tell Herod that Salome was busy making all sorts of plots against him; and she had also sent him a copy of the letter to her

141 mistress purporting to come from Salome. Acme was a Jewess by birth but a slave of Caesar's wife Julia, and she had acted in this way out of friendship for Antipater, who had bribed her generously to assist his evil designs against his father and his aunt.

142 Herod was appalled by the enormity of Antipater's wickedness and felt the urge to dispose of him at once for stirring up such turmoil, and for plotting not only against himself but against his sister and for corrupting the household of Caesar. He was egged on by Salome, who beat her breast and bade him kill her if her behaviour could lend

143 any credence to such charges. Herod then sent for his son and questioned him, telling him to speak fearlessly if he had any defence to offer; and when he remained dumb he put it to him that he stood convicted of every crime with which he was charged, and asked him at least to name his accomplices immediately.

144 Antipater laid the entire blame on Antiphilus, and named no one else. Heartbroken, Herod's first impulse was to send his son to Caesar in Rome to stand trial for

145 his plotting. But afterwards, anxious that Antipater might find a way out of his danger with the help of his friends, he kept him in chains as before, and again sent off envoys with a letter accusing his son and exposing Acme's role as his accomplice, and with copies of the intercepted letters.

Sedition in Jerusalem

146 And so the envoys, fully briefed with what to say under questioning and bearing the letters, hurried on their way to Rome. But the king fell ill and made a will, bequeathing his kingdom to his youngest son* out of hatred for Archelaus and Philip: Antipater's slanders had proved effective. To Caesar he left a thousand talents, and to Julia, Caesar's wife, and to his children, friends and freed-

147 men five hundred talents. He made grants of money, revenues and lands to his own sons and to their sons, and settled a large inheritance on his sister Salome, who had remained loyal to him through everything and had never ventured to do him harm.

148 His despair of recovery – he was in fact about seventy years old – made him grow savage, and everyone smarted under his unbridled and bitter outbursts of rage. His mood was caused by the belief that he was despised and that the nation took pleasure in his misfortunes, a belief that found confirmation in an uprising against him organised by some popular leaders.

149 The occasion was as follows. Judas, the son of Seri-phaeus, and Matthias, the son of Margalothus, were Jews of great learning and unrivalled as interpreters of the ancestral laws. They were also held in great affection by the people as educators of the youth, since all serious

150 students of moral virtue frequented their company day after day. When they learned that there was no cure for the king's illness, they incited the young people to tear down the structures built by the king in contravention of the Law of their fathers, and so win from the Law the rewards of their piety. They maintained that it was obvi-ously his temerity in fashioning such things in defiance of the Law's prescriptions that had condemned him to a life of such extraordinary misfortune, and to his illness in particular.

151 It was indeed true that some of Herod's projects had been in breach of the Law, and for those he incurred the censure of Judas and Matthias and their disciples. Over the great gate of the Temple the king had constructed at extravagant expense a votive offering in the form of a

great golden eagle,* although the Law forbids its adher-
ents to entertain the idea of erecting images or dedicating
effigies of living creatures.

152   The learned teachers therefore urged their disciples to
pull down the eagle, assuring them that, whatever the
danger of the death sentence, those who were prepared to
die to preserve and safeguard the tradition of their fathers
would profit more from the virtue they displayed in death
than from the pleasure of living. They would earn for
themselves an eternal fame, celebrated by their contemporaries and leaving to future generations the everlasting

153   memorial of their lives. And if death was inescapable even
for the sheltered life, how much better to strive after virtue,
and accept their fate with honour and renown when they

154   departed this life! To die in a noble cause, from which
danger was inseparable, was a far lighter fate, and the
good name it would win them would live on to benefit
their sons and any relatives, whether men or women, who
survived them.

155   Such were the sentiments with which they roused the
youth, and when a rumour reached them that the king had
died it served to strengthen the teachers' hand. At midday,
therefore, when the Temple area was crowded with visitors, they went up and pulled the eagle down, using axes
to hack it off.

156   When the king's captain was brought news of the
attempt, he construed their purpose more seriously than
the action merited and, arriving with a large body of men,
strong enough to deal with the numbers intent on demol-
ishing the effigy, he fell on them and took them by
surprise. As is the way of crowds, it was a thoughtless
whim rather than the confidence of foresight that had
made them bold, and they were in disarray and unpre-

157   pared to help themselves. He captured no fewer than forty
of the young men, who had bravely awaited his attack
when the rest of the crowd took to flight, and with them
the instigators of the bold venture, Judas and Matthias,
who had thought it dishonourable to give way at his
approach; and he took them to the king.

158   When they came to him, the king asked them if they
had dared to demolish the offering he had set up, and they

replied, 'We did, but our intentions and our actions were inspired by a virtue very proper in a man. We have acted in defence of principles which, by God's consent, we hold

159 in trust and which are of deep concern to us as disciples of the Law. It can be no cause for surprise if we regard your decrees as less worthy of respect than the laws that Moses bequeathed to us, and which he wrote on the prompting and instruction of God. We shall bear death or whatever punishment you may inflict on us with pleasure, knowing that it is not for any fault of ours but for our love of piety that death keeps us company.'

160 They all made this response, showing the same boldness in their speech as when they ventured on their exploit. The king put them in chains and dispatched them to Jericho,

161 where he summoned the Jewish magistrates, and when they arrived he held an assembly in the amphitheatre. Unable to stand and lying on a couch, he recounted his strenuous efforts on their behalf, and in particular his

162 rebuilding of the Temple at great personal expense; whereas the Hasmonaeans, he said, in their reign of a hundred and twenty-five years had been unable to honour God with any comparable achievement. He had also

163 adorned the Temple with magnificent dedicatory offerings, and in return for these works he had cherished the hope that even after his death he would leave behind a memorial of himself and an illustrious name. At this point he began to shout that even in his lifetime they had not shrunk from insulting him. In broad daylight and with the people looking on, they had had the insolence to lay hands on the offering he had set up and had torn it down – an outrage professedly committed against himself but which on closer scrutiny was proved to be an act of sacrilege.

164 Because of his savage mood the magistrates, who were afraid that he might take vengeance on them in his rage, declared that none of this had been done with their consent and that in their opinion it was an appropriate case for punishment. Herod, while dealing rather leniently with the others, stripped the high priest Matthias of the priesthood for his share of responsibility and appointed his wife's brother Joazar* to be high priest.

165 It was during the high priesthood of this Matthias that

another high priest was appointed for a single day, on
166 which the Jews observe a fast. This came about because
on the eve of the fast-day Matthias, a priest, dreamed
during the night that he had had intercourse with a
woman, and so was debarred from performing his priestly
duties, and his relative Joseph, the son of Ellemus, served
as priest in his place.

167   After removing this Matthias from the high priesthood,
Herod burned alive the other Matthias, who had incited
the uprising, along with some of his supporters. On the
same night there was an eclipse of the moon.*

The Execution of Antipater and Herod's Death

168 Herod's illness became increasingly severe, as God punished him for his unlawful acts. He had a mild fever,
showing little evidence of inflammation to the touch but
169 accompanied by serious internal disorder, one of the symptoms being a desperate and compulsive urge to get relief
by scratching himself. He suffered ulceration of the bow-
els, with acute intestinal pains, and an effusion of colour-
less fluid around the feet. He had a similar disorder of the
abdomen, and what is more, a gangrene of the genitals
that produced worms. He had difficulty in getting his
breath when sitting upright, and his breathing was
extremely unpleasant because of the offensive nature of
the exhalation and his constant gasping. And in every limb
he experienced convulsions that became unbearably
violent.*

170   The soothsayers and men whose wisdom qualified them
to pronounce on these matters interpreted the king's condition as a punishment inflicted on him by God for his
171 great impiety. Yet though his sufferings were beyond
bearing Herod still entertained hopes of recovery and
summoned his doctors, fully resolved to try whatever
remedies they suggested. He crossed the River Jordan and
bathed in the warm springs of Callirrhoe, whose waters
run into Lake Asphaltophoros* and are good to drink in
addition to their other beneficial properties. His physicians
172 decided to warm his body there and sat him in a tub of
oil, but he fainted and they thought him dead. The cries

of grief from his servants brought him round, but he finally despaired of his survival and gave orders for money to be distributed to the soldiers, fifty drachmas to each 173 man, and made large donations besides to their officers and to his own friends.

He then returned to Jericho, where a black mood took hold of him and made him feel such bitterness towards everyone alike that even on his death-bed he conceived the 174 following plan. Jewish men of note had come to Jericho on his order from the length and breadth of the country, and they were there in large numbers; the entire nation had been called on and everyone had obeyed his decree, since disobedience to his instructions meant death. In a mad fit of rage against them all, whether they were innocent or had given him some cause, he locked them all 175 together in the hippodrome. He then sent for his sister Salome and her husband Alexas and told them that the pains that afflicted every part of his body were now so severe that he was close to death. Death itself, he said, he could bear as the common experience of humanity, but that he should die unlamented and without the customary 176 mourning for a king was very distressing to him. He was well aware of the feelings of the Jews. They prayed for his death and would be overjoyed when it came – even in his lifetime they had been eager to rebel and treated his ordinances with insolence.

177   So the two of them had a duty, he suggested, to determine some means of relief for him from the hurt that this caused him, and if they would agree to fall in with his own plan then he would have a grand funeral, such as no other king had ever had, and the whole nation would be in mourning, their mockery and laughter at him turned to 178 heartfelt lamentation. He then proposed that when they saw that he had breathed his last, they should surround the hippodrome with soldiers, still ignorant of his death – which was not to be announced to the people until his plan was carried out – and order them to shoot the men confined there. By destroying them all in this way they could not fail to make him glad on two counts: his last instructions would be fulfilled, and he would be honoured 179 with a memorable show of mourning. He sobbed aloud as

he made this request, appealing to their family loyalty and faith in God, and charging them not to let him go unhonoured; and they agreed not to disregard his wishes.

180   Even if we accept his earlier reprisals against his family as acts of self-preservation, we can see from these last instructions at least that the man's character had no trace

181   of humanity in it. The proof is that, even at the very point of death, he planned to leave the whole nation bereaved of their dearest ones and in a state of mourning, by giving orders that one member of every household should be put to death, innocent though they were of any offence against him and accused of no other crimes – and that at a moment when men with some pretence to virtue normally set aside their hatred, even towards those who have deserved their enmity.

182   While he was giving these instructions to his relatives, a letter arrived from Rome from the envoys sent to Caesar, the substance of which was that Caesar had put Acme to death in anger at her complicity in Antipater's crimes, and that as for Antipater himself he left it to Herod's judgement, as his father and his king, whether he preferred to send him into exile or to execute him.

183   When Herod heard the letter read he briefly revived in his pleasure at its contents, elated by the death of Acme and the authority given him to punish his son; but then his pains grew much worse and in utter dejection he began to refuse his food. He asked for an apple and a knife – it

184   had always been his habit to peel his own apple and cut it up to eat – and on being given the knife he gave a look round with the intention of stabbing himself; and he would have done so if his cousin Achiab, with a loud cry, had not stopped him by seizing his hand. His shout was echoed by cries of lamentation throughout the palace, and there was uproar when people believed that the king had passed away.

185   Antipater, who was convinced that his father was really dead, began to talk with a new assurance, supposing that he was now completely freed from his shackles and that he could take the throne for himself without an effort. He discussed his release with the jailer, promising him handsome recompense on the spot and in the future, as if the

186 time was now right for such negotiations; but the jailer not only turned down his request but revealed his intention

187 to the king, with extra details of his own invention. Herod, who already felt no special affection for his son, cried aloud on hearing the jailer's words and, though at the point of death, he beat his head, raised himself on his elbow and sent some of his bodyguard with orders to waste not a moment but kill Antipater at once, and bury him without honour in Hyrcania.

188 He then changed his mind again and made a new will, designating Antipas, to whom he had left his throne, to be tetrarch of Galilee and Peraea, and bequeathing his king-

189 dom to Archelaus. Gaulanitis, Trachonitis, Batanaea and Paneas he assigned as a tetrarchy to his son Philip, a full brother* of Archelaus, and Jamnea, Azotus and Phasaelis

190 to his sister Salome, along with five hundred thousand pieces of coined silver. He also made provision for all his other relatives, leaving them gifts of money and the payment of revenues to keep them comfortably off. To Caesar he left ten million of pieces of coined silver, together with vessels of gold and silver and some luxurious articles of clothing, and to Julia, Caesar's wife, and some others five million pieces of silver.

191 After doing this, he died, four days after executing his son Antipater. He had reigned for thirty-four years from the time when he put Antigonus to death, and for thirty-seven years from the time when he was proclaimed king by the Romans. He was a man of indiscriminate cruelty, with an ungovernable temper and a contempt for justice, yet fortune favoured him as much as any man. Born a

192 commoner, he rose to become king, and though beset by innumerable dangers he contrived to escape them all and lived to a great age. In his domestic life and relations with his sons he considered himself very fortunate for his success in defeating those he judged to be his enemies, but in my opinion this was his great misfortune.

193 Before news of the king's death got abroad Salome and Alexas dismissed the men summoned to the hippodrome and sent them home, telling them that it was the king's command that they should leave for their own fields and attend to their own business; and by taking this action

194 they did the nation the greatest service. When the king's death became generally known, the two of them assembled the army in the amphitheatre at Jericho, and first of all read out a letter that Herod had written to the soldiers, thanking them for their loyalty and goodwill to him and requesting the same suppport for his son Archelaus, to
195 whom he left his kingdom. Next, Ptolemy, who was entrusted with the king's seal, read out his will, which had to await ratification when Caesar had perused it. A shout went up at once as they acclaimed Archelaus as their king, and the soldiers and their officers advanced in their companies to promise him their loyal support, and called on God to help him.

196 They then made preparations for the king's burial. Archelaus made it his concern to give his father a magnificent funeral and brought out all the royal ornaments to
197 accompany the cortège. Herod was carried on a golden bier, studded with precious stones of various colours and draped with a purple covering. His body was wrapped in crimson robes, wearing a diadem surmounted by a golden crown, and by his right hand lay his sceptre.

198 Around the bier walked his sons and his many relatives, and behind them came the army organised according to their nationalities and titles as follows: first his bodyguard, next the Thracians, after them the Germans, and then the
199 Gauls, all of them in battle array.* Behind these came the whole army, marching as if to war and led by their company commanders and subordinate officers. They were followed by five hundred servants carrying spices. And they went eight stades towards Herodeion,* where his burial took place by his own command.

This, then, was the manner of Herod's death.

NOTES

ABBREVIATIONS
JW Jewish War
JA Jewish Antiquities

Book XIV

p. 3 Pompey: in 63 BC, while organising Syria as a Roman province, Pompey took Jerusalem by force to depose Aristobulus II and reinstate his brother Hyrcanus II as high priest and ethnarch of the Jews.

p. 3 eldest son Phasael: Antipater and his Arab wife Cypros had four sons and a daughter: Phasael, Herod, Joseph, Pheroras and Salome.

p. 3 Herod . . . fifteen: Herod must have been about twenty-five in 47 BC, as he was about seventy at his death in 4 BC (XVII, line 148). The text may be corrupt, but if it is sound, Josephus exaggerates Herod's youth.

p. 4 Sextus Caesar . . . Syria: Sextus Caesar became governor of Syria in the summer of 47 BC.

pp. 4–5 He killed . . . Sanhedrin: this passage assumes that the Sanhedrin was the supreme judicial body of the Jewish state. The Sanhedrin appears elsewhere in the history of this period, sometimes with an administrative or legislative role, but its precise functions, composition, competence and procedures are all uncertain.

p. 6 he postponed . . . day: Josephus's account of the trial, as in *JW*, does not make it clear whether Herod was formally acquitted or the trial postponed.

p. 6 Coele-Syria: *JW*, i, 213 says 'Coele-Syria and Samaria'.

p. 7 a major war . . . him: in the autumn of 45 BC. The Caesarian legions were commanded by C. Antistius Vetus, who was succeeded early in 44 BC by L. Statius Murcus.

p. 8 three years and six months: three years and seven months elapsed between Caesar's defeat of Pompey at Pharsalia (9 August 48 BC) and Caesar's murder (15 March 44 BC).

p. 9 This done: 43 BC

p. 9 festival: probably the Festival of Tabernacles in October 43 BC

p. 10 captured Laodicea: in the summer of 43 BC, after besieging Dolabella, Antony's fellow consul in the previous year, who had been sent to govern Syria for the Caesarians. Dolabella committed suicide.

p. 10 The departure . . . Syria: early in 42 BC

p. 11 Ptolemy . . . marriage: Ptolemy was prince of Chalcis in Lebanon. He was married to Alexandra, sister of Antigonus, the son of Hyrcanus's brother and rival Aristobulus.

p. 11 daughter of Alexander: Mariamme I

p. 11 Cassius . . . Caesar: October 42 BC. From here onwards in the narrative, 'Caesar' refers to Octavian, the adopted son and heir of Julius and later the Emperor Augustus (a title he took in 27 BC). At line 280 above, he is called 'the young Caesar'.

p. 11 Hyrcanus . . . kingship: the Romans designated Hyrcanus as ethnarch, but the Jews called him king.

p. 13 me and Dolabella: Antony and Dolabella, as consuls in 44 BC, and Dolabella as governor of Syria in 43 BC, confirmed the privileges granted to the Jews by Julius Caesar, absolving them from military service and protecting their religious customs.

p. 14 Cleopatra . . . love: Cleopatra had been charged with aiding Cassius, and came to defend herself in the late summer of 41 BC, sailing up the River Cydnus adorned as Aphrodite in a golden barge.

p. 15 Daphne: a suburb of Antioch

p. 15 Gabinius: as governor of Syria in 57–55 BC, Gabinius, with the help of Antipater, had defeated an uprising against Hyrcanus led by Aristobulus's son Alexander.

p. 15 Two years later: the spring of 40 BC

p. 17 Freemen: an élite corps, since most of the Parthian soldiers were slaves

p. 18 Hyrcanus's daughter: Alexandra, the mother of Mariamme I

p. 19 sixty stades: about seven miles. A *stade* was between 195 and 220 yards.

p. 20 the law ... defects: *Leviticus* 21: 17ff.

p. 22 set sail ... Pamphylia: late in 40 BC

p. 22 Antipater's ... Egypt: in the autumn of 48 BC Julius Caesar pursued Pompey to Egypt, where Pompey was murdered. Caesar became involved in a war with Ptolemy XIII, and was supported by Hyrcanus and Antipater, who led Jewish troops to assist him and his ally Mithridates.

p. 23 original ... them: he had assisted his father, Aristobulus II, against Hyrcanus.

p. 23 wife's brother ... mother's: Aristobulus III, son of Alexander, the son of Aristobulus II, and of Alexandra, daughter of Hyrcanus II

p. 23 hundred ... Pollio: in December 40 BC. The 184th Olympiad ended in July 40 BC.

p. 25 Idumaean ... half-Jew: The Idumaeans, south of Judaea, had been forced to adopt the Jewish religion by Hyrcanus I (135–104 BC), but conversions were either valid or not, and the accusation that they were 'half-Jewish' is theologically impossible and no more than an insult.

p. 25 The verbal ... attack: the text of this sentence is suspect. The translation follows the sense of the parallel passage in *JW*, i, 296.

p. 26 winter quarters: the winter of 39–38 BC

p. 29 In the meantime ... routed: June 38 BC

p. 30 Samosata: held by Antiochus, king of Commagene, an ally of the Parthians

p. 32 but were ... Romans: text emended to the sense of *JW*, i, 332. The manuscripts here have 'They frightened away the Romans'.

p. 33 When ... Jerusalem: spring, 37 BC

p. 34 sabbatical year: during a sabbatical year the ground was not tilled. The siege began in the spring of 37 BC, but it is disputed whether the sabbatical year extended from October 38 to October 37 or from October 37 to October 36, and it is uncertain which of these alternatives Josephus had in mind. The interpretation, accuracy and consistency of Josephus' references to the dates of the siege and fall of

Jerusalem are a complex issue (see, for example, Schürer, i, p. 284, n. 11; and Loeb, vii, p. 196, n. A and p. 694, n. A). In the next sentence Josephus suggests that the siege lasted barely three months, but at *JW*, i, 351 he says it lasted five months.

p. 35 'Antigone':   the feminine form of Antigonus, and the name of a famous heroine of tragic drama

p. 36 consulship . . . Gallus: 37 BC

p. 36 Olympiad: the Olympiad ended on 30 June 37 BC.

p. 36 day of the Fast: this appears to refer to the Day of Atonement, which fell on 3 October in 37 BC. However, there is considerable doubt as to the day and the month, which may have been July (see Schürer, i, p. 284, n. 11, and Loeb, vii, p. 700, n. D). Pompey's capture of the city in 63 BC was twenty-six, not twenty-seven, years earlier. It too occurred 'on the day of the Fast', but Josephus' pagan sources may have meant by this the Sabbath, not the Atonement (see Loeb, vii, p. 480, n. C).

p. 36 this was done: Antigonus was beheaded by Antony at Antioch (XV, line 8).

Book XV

p. 37 It was . . . them all: according to XIV, line 172, it was Samaias who spoke against Herod.

p. 37 sabbatical . . . earth: see note above, p. 34.

p. 38 triumph: to celebrate his defeat of the Parthians

p. 40 Aristobulus . . . Alexander: Aristobulus II, Hyrcanus's brother and rival, and his son Alexander were killed by the Pompeians in 49 BC.

p. 42 Antiochus Epiphanes: the Seleucid king who reigned at Antioch 175–163 BC. His attempts to hellenise the Jews provoked a revival of Jewish nationalism and the rise of the Hasmonaean dynasty.

p. 42 Hyrcanus: in 67 BC Hyrcanus ceded the royal power to his brother, after being defeated in battle.

p. 43 feast of Tabernacles: probably October 35 BC

p. 45 Laodicea: Antony was about to launch a new attack on the

Parthians, early in 34 BC. In the event he invaded and conquered Armenia.

p. 49 her brother: Ptolemy XIV, who died soon after Cleopatra returned to Egypt from Rome in 44 BC

p. 49 Lysanias: Lysanias, the ruler of Ituraea, had been an ally of Antigonus, the son of Aristobulus II.

p. 51 Battle of Actium: the naval battle was fought on 2 September 31 BC.

p. 55 messengers ... God: probably a reference to the Jewish prophets (see Feldman (1984), p. 473)

p. 59 Lake Asphaltitis: the Dead Sea. It is also called Asphaltophoros at XVII, line 171.

p. 60 eighty-one years old: an exaggeration. Hyrcanus' mother, Salome Alexandra, married his father, Alexander Jannaeus, after the death of her first husband, Aristobulus I, in 103 BC. Hyrcanus was executed in 30 BC.

p. 61 mother ... reign: 76 BC. Alexander bequeathed his kingdom to his queen in preference to their sons, Hyrcanus and Aristobulus.

p. 61 mother's death: 67 BC

p. 61 Restored ... Antigonus: Hyrcanus was reinstated by Pompey in 63 BC and deposed by Antigonus in 40 BC, a reign of twenty-three years.

p. 63 Quintus Didius: governor of Syria in 31–30 BC, he had prevented gladiators trained by Antony at Cyzicus from going to his support after the Battle of Actium.

p. 63 Alexas: sent to confirm Herod in his loyalty to Antony, he had deserted to Octavian, but was put to death by him.

p. 66 Caesar ... Egypt: the end of August 30 BC. Antony and Cleopatra committed suicide after being defeated by Octavian at Alexandria.

p. 67 father: a mistake. Hyrcanus was her grandfather, not her father. Her brother was Aristobulus III.

p. 71 Hyrcanus ... Jews: see note on p. 25.

p. 73 family of Hyrcanus: the relationship of these men to Hyrcanus is not known.

p. 73 *thymelikoi*:   these perhaps performed musical stage-plays.

p. 76 fortress . . . by him: cf. XV, lines 403–9.

p. 76 Sebaste: in honour of Augustus, *Sebastos* being the Greek for Augustus

p. 76 Caesarea: see XV, lines 331–41

p. 76 Great Plain: the Plain of Esdraelon, between Samaria and Galilee

p. 77 twenty stades: a little over two miles

p. 77 thirteenth . . . reign: 25–24 BC

p. 79 cor . . . bushels: the *cor* was a Hebrew measure, approximately equivalent to 370 litres or 11 bushels, i.e. roughly 7, not 10, Attic bushels (*medimnoi*).

p. 80 daughter . . . Jerusalem: her name, like that of Herod's second wife, was Mariamme.

p. 80 fortress: it was named Herodeion.

p. 82 Drusus . . . young: Nero Claudius Drusus, 38–9 BC, the son of Augustus's wife Livia by her first husband Tiberius Claudius Nero. He was the brother of Augustus's successor, Tiberius.

p. 83 Trachonitis . . . Auranitis: the territory of these three districts is the Biblical Bashan and Gilead.

p. 83 Lysanias: killed by Antony at the instigation of Cleopatra (see XV, 92)

p. 84 Zenodorus . . . eparchy: coins of Zenodorus describe him as 'tetrarch and high priest' (Schürer, i, p. 566). In the hellenised east of the Roman empire 'tetrarch' had become a general title for a local dynast.

p. 85 seventeenth . . . reign: 20 BC

p. 86 mountain: Mount Hermon

p. 87 Essenes . . . Pythagoras: Josephus gave a detailed account of the Essenes in *JW* ii, 119–61. The hypothesis that the sectarian Jews who produced the Dead Sea Scrolls were Essenes is plausible but debated. Josephus does not state explicitly that the Essenes were historically influenced by Pythagoreanism, and the question is disputed. The similarities he has in mind may include reverence for the sun, belief in immortality, and various esoteric rules and rituals.

p. 89 Temple: the Temple was rebuilt in the time of Zerubbabel, Jewish governor of Judaea under Persian domination (see following note).

pp. 89–90 Cyrus ... Macedonians: Cyrus the Great, founder of the Persian empire (559–529 BC) annexed Palestine as part of the former Babylonian empire. He allowed the captive Jews to return to rebuild their Temple. Darius I reigned 521–486 BC. 'Macedonians' refers to Alexander the Great and his Seleucid successors at Antioch.

p. 90 cubits: a *cubit* was about 20 inches.

p. 90 In ... again: King Agrippa II imported timber to underpin and raise the height of the Temple, but it was put to military use in the Roman siege of Jerusalem in AD 70.

p. 92 Fortress: it was in the north-west corner of the Temple area, where Herod built his fortress Antonia, and had been built about 134 BC by Hyrcanus I.

p. 92 Vitellius ... Jerusalem: AD 36

p. 92 The Jews ... Syria: Agrippa I ruled in Judaea AD 41–44. Cassius Longinus was governor of Syria AD 45–50. The younger Agrippa, son of Agrippa I, was to reign in the north of Palestine as Agrippa II AD 50–c.100.

p. 92 valley: the Valley of Tyropoeon or Cheesemakers (*JW*, v, 140)

p. 92 suburb: the suburb of Bezetha

p. 93 ravine: the Valley of Hinnom, or Gehenna

p. 93 Royal ... length: it stretched from the Kedron Valley to the Tyropoeon.

p. 93 first ... court: the first court is the Court of Gentiles, the second the Court of Israel.

p. 94 King ... courts: this is strange – we might expect 'the third of these courts', i.e. the Court of Priests.

p. 94 Temple ... scale: the summer of 18 BC

Book XVI

p. 106 Herod ... Rome: 12 BC

p. 112 The entire ... reign: 10–9 BC. At XV, line 341, Josephus says that Sebaste took twelve years to complete, which would put the start of the work in 22 BC. The 'tenth year' of the present passage is less likely.

p. 112 These games ... years: they were called the Actium Games, in honour of Octavian's (Augustus's) victory in 31 BC.

p. 113 Plain of Capharsaba: the Plain of Sharon

p. 115 Hyrcanus ... silver: Hyrcanus I, during the siege of Jerusalem in 135–134 BC

p. 116 We ... honours: Josephus tells us in his autobiography that his family belonged to the first of the twenty-four priestly classes, and that his maternal grandfather had married the daughter of the Hasmonaean high priest Jonathan (161–143 BC).

p. 117 King's daughter: Salampsio, a daughter of Herod and Mariamme I

p. 117 son of Phasael: his name, like his father's, was Phasael.

p. 128 Saturninus and Volumnius: the Roman governor of Syria was C. Sentius Saturninus (c.9–6 BC). Volumnius was his equestrian subordinate.

p. 133 He was informed: words are missing here in the manuscripts. According to *JW* (i, 532–3), Euaratus was a close friend of Alexander who assured Herod on oath that he had heard no evidence of his son's disloyalty.

p. 137 Berytus: modern Beirut

p. 140 a law ... death: *Deuteronomy*, 21: 18–21

p. 144 strangling: the punishment also inflicted on Hyrcanus, strangling is one of four forms of capital punishment recognised by the *Mishnah*, the earliest extant corpus of rabbinic law, compiled c.AD 200, the other forms being stoning, burning and beheading. The crimes for which strangling was prescribed included bruising a parent and insubordination to supreme authority, but these prescriptions were only theoretical since rabbis lacked capital jurisdiction, and their relationship to Jewish law in Herodian Judaea is unknown.

p. 144 **Fate . . . Law:** in *JA*, xviii, 12–15, Josephus attributes to the Pharisees the view that everything is brought about by Fate, but that this is compatible with the exercise of human free will and moral responsibility. In fact, the Stoic concept of Fate and the Hebrew concept of Providence are not identical, but Josephus follows his usual practice of assimilating Jewish and Greek beliefs.

p. 145 **How . . . crime:** Herod would have been about sixty-five at this time (?7 BC).

Book XVII

p. 147 **her daughter . . . uncle:** the daughter was Berenice, and Antipater's uncle was named Theudion.

p. 147 **Salome's . . . Calleas:** the son of Calleas was Alexas, but the name of Salome's second daughter is unknown.

p. 147 **Alexander's wife:** Glaphyra

p. 147 **two . . . Glaphyra:** the boys' names were Tigranes and Alexander.

p. 147 **three . . . girls:** the boys were Herod (of Chalcis), Agrippa and Aristobulus; the girls Herodias and Mariamme. It was Herodias in the New Testament who ordered her daughter Salome to demand the head of John the Baptist (e.g. *Mark* 6: 17, 19, 22).

p. 148 **Alexander's . . . Antipater:** the names are unknown.

p. 148 **the two . . . Herod:** Mariamme married Antipater's son, and Herodias married Herod's own son, Herod, whose mother was Mariamme II, daughter of Simon the high priest. Herodias later married Herod Antipas, son of Malthace, the tetrarch of Galilee who beheaded John the Baptist.

p. 148 **mother:** Doris.

p. 148 **daughter . . . cousin:** the names are unknown.

p. 148 **Samaritan woman:** Malthace

p. 148 **king's nephew:** he was the son of Herod's brother, Joseph.

p. 149 **eldest daughters:** Cypros and Salampsio

p. 149 **Philip:** Philip was tetrarch of Batanaea and adjacent districts 4 BC–AD 34.

p. 149 **Agrippa . . . name:** see note on p. 92.

p. 150 **Jacimus:** Jacimus and his son Philip held office under Agrippa II.

p. 150·**even . . . daughters:** the translation here adopts an emendation conforming to the sense of the parallel passages at *JW*, i, 568 and 571. In the manuscripts it is Pheroras who resents the insults to his own daughters.

p. 157 **her son . . . successor:** this was Herod, the son of Mariamme II.

p. 158 **governor of Syria:** *c.*6–4 BC

p. 167 **youngest son:** Antipas, a son by Malthace

p. 168 **eagle:** early Greek temples of Zeus had the pediment decorated with an eagle as a symbol of the God (Loeb, ii, p. 308, n. A), and the king of birds was an emblem of Roman power. An eagle also appears on a late coin of Herod's reign (Schürer, i, p. 312, n. 85).

p. 169 **Joazar:** he was a son of Boethus and brother of Mariamme II.

p. 170 **On the . . . moon:** 13 March 4 BC.

p. 170 **Herod's . . . violent:** for modern diagnoses of Herod's terminal illness, see Feldman (1984), pp. 298–9.

p. 170 **Lake Asphaltophoros:** the Dead Sea (cf. note on p. 59)

p. 173 **full brother:** a mistake. Philip was the son of Cleopatra, and Archelaus of Malthace (cf. XVII, lines 20–21).

p. 174 **army . . . array:** Herod used foreign mercenaries to put down internal uprisings as well as for defence against foreign enemies.

p. 174 **Herodeion:** this Herodeion, 60 stades south of Jerusalem, and about 200 stades from Jericho, is described at XV, lines 323–5. The modern name is Jebel el-Fereidis.

SUGGESTIONS FOR FURTHER READING

On Josephus

Attridge, H. W., 'Josephus and his Works', in M. Stone (ed.), *Jewish Writings of the Second Temple Period* (Assen and Philadelphia, 1984), pp. 185–232

Bilde, P., *Flavius Josephus between Jerusalem and Rome: His Life, his Works and their Importance* (Sheffield, 1988)

Cohen, S. J. D., *Josephus in Galilee and Rome. His Vita and Development as a Historian* (Leiden, 1979)

Feldman, L. H. *Josephus and Modern Scholarship 1937–1980* (Berlin and New York, 1984)

Laqueur, R., *Der jüdische Historiker Flavius Josephus* (Giessen, 1920)

Parente, F. and J. Sievers (eds), *Josephus and the History of the Greco-Roman Period* (Leiden, 1994)

Rajak, T., *Josephus: The Historian and his Society* (London, 1983)

Rengstorf, K. H. (ed.), *A Complete Concordance to Flavius Josephus* (vols i–iv) (Leiden, 1973–83)

Shutt, R. J. H., *Studies in Josephus* (London, 1961)

Schreckenberg, H., *Rezeptiongeschichtliche und textkritische Untersuchungen zu Flavius Josephus* (Leiden, 1977)

Thackeray, H. St J., *Josephus the Man and the Historian* (New York, 1929)

Thackeray, H. St J., R. Marcus, A. Wikgren and L. H. Feldman, *Josephus* (Loeb Classical Texts, vols. i–ix: Cambridge, Mass. and London, 1926–65)

On Herod

Richardson, P., *Herod: King of the Jews and Friend of the Romans* (University of South Carolina Press: Columbia, South Carolina, 1996)

Schalit, A., *König Herodes. Der Mann und sein Werk* (Berlin, 1969)

Schürer, E., *The History of the Jewish People in the Age of Jesus*

Christ, 175 BC–AD 135, 3 vols, rev. and ed. G. Vermes, F. Millar, M. Black and M. Goodman (Edinburgh, 1973–87), vol. I, pp. 275–329

Smallwood, E. M., *The Jews under Roman Rule from Pompey to Diocletian* (Leiden, 1976)